FROM

Bullied

TO

Blessed

Keys to Overcoming Obstacles in Your
Life & Learning to Enjoy the Ride

DAVID BESCH

WESTBOW
P R E S S®
A DIVISION OF THOMAS NELSON
& ZONDERVAN

WestBow Press books may be ordered through booksellers or by contacting:

WestBow Press
A Division of Thomas Nelson & Zondervan
1663 Liberty Drive
Bloomington, IN 47403
www.westbowpress.com
1 (866) 928-1240

Cover Photo by Tallie Johnson Photography of Colorado.

ISBN: 978-1-9736-0909-4 (sc)
ISBN: 978-1-9736-0910-0 (hc)
ISBN: 978-1-9736-0908-7 (e)

Library of Congress Control Number: 2017917994

Printed in the United States of America.

WestBow Press rev. date: 2/06/2018

Contents

Preface

Bully "a blustering browbeating person; especially one habitually cruel to others who are weaker"[1]

Bullying "acts or written or spoken words intended to intimidate or harass a person or to cause physical harm to a person or his or her property"[2]

"Your beginnings will seem humble, so prosperous will your future be." Job 8:7 (NIV)

Bullying has been linked to suicide, low self-esteem, shame, guilt, pains from the past and peer pressure – this does not define who you are because you are "fearfully and wonderfully made" Psalms 139:14 – (KJV) and God has a great plan for your life – "plans to prosper you and not to harm you, plans to give you hope and a future" Jeremiah 29:11- (NIV)

Prevention and intervention are keys to dealing with bullies. Finding strong friends, mentors, family, clergy, teachers and sometimes even law enforcement intervention is necessary to stop bullying. Don't make the greatest mistake to be selfish and hurtful to others by taking your own life. Like many, I considered it and am so thankful I didn't go through with it because of how blessed my life has turned out today.

David Besch

Introduction

To all who have ever felt bullied at any time in their life, I pray this book will bring new insight to what you can actually achieve and overcome. Whether as a child or as an adult, most of us have encountered bullies in some form or fashion. I understand the emotions, hurt, shame and embarrassment I've experienced may not be to the same extent that some others have had, just as I know there is much worse than what I've gone through. Hang on, there's a better road ahead. Where you are today is not your final destiny. God has much more for you and it doesn't involve bullies robbing you of your peace of mind and stealing your joy. The past pains, shame, guilt, and hurts do not have to determine your future life. You can have inner calm in the midst of the storms of life and experience an abundant life of joy, peace, favor, prosperity, and health.

It's time to stand up for yourself and have more self-respect and dignity. You are made in the image of Almighty God the creator of the universe! You are full of greatness and unlimited potential is inside of you. You have what it takes to be great and not to live like a doormat and be stepped on and abused, whether that is verbal or physical. Sometimes it's the soft answer that turns the wrath of the bully away, other times we must take further action. We need help from others and God's grace and strength. You already possess the answers, now take action and appropriate it in your life.

"Do not be afraid; you will not be put to shame. Do not fear disgrace; you will not be humiliated. You will forget the shame of your youth" Isaiah 54:4 (NIV)

"No weapon forged against you will prevail, and you will refute every tongue that accuses you. This is the heritage of the servants of the LORD, and this is their vindication from me," declares the LORD." Isaiah 54:17 (NIV)

"Although you have been forsaken and hated, with no one traveling through, I will make you the everlasting pride and the joy of all generations." Isaiah 60:15 (NIV)

"Instead of your shame you will receive a double portion, and instead of disgrace you will rejoice in your inheritance. And so you will inherit a double portion in your land, and everlasting joy will be yours." Isaiah 61:7 (NIV)

"Ask and it will be given to you; seek and you will find; knock and the door will be opened to you." Matthew 7:7 (NIV)

"Have I not commanded you? Be strong and courageous. Do not be afraid; do not be discouraged, for the LORD your God will be with you wherever you go." Joshua 1:9 (NIV)

"So do not fear, for I am with you; do not be dismayed, for I am your God. I will strengthen you and help you; I will uphold you with my righteous right hand." Isaiah 41:10 (NIV)

From the Author

This book was written with the objective of helping readers understand that the past is over and your best days are yet to come. You cannot change the past, but there is a way to deal with your painful memories and emotions that exist deep inside the small crevasses of your heart. Isaiah 43:18-19 says, "Forget the former things; do not dwell on the past. See, I am doing a new thing! Now it springs up; do you not perceive it? I am making a way in the wilderness and streams in the wasteland." You can release the past and step forward to a brighter future! Don't let low self-esteem from a bully's powerless words limit you any longer. You have greatness inside of you and can achieve your greatest dreams and desires.

You can reprogram the thought patterns in your mind and replace those toxic memories that continue to surface and haunt you. It's time to move forward to your destiny. You can, however, learn from experience and mistakes. I heard a teacher once ask how we learn. The answer was by making mistakes. Many of us have made the mistake in allowing others to bully us. It may be classmates, teachers, siblings, coaches or bosses. Racism and prejudice is one of the worst types of bullying. This has scarred many young and old individuals over the centuries. It has impacted our entire culture in such a negative and toxic way that has produced hate, anger and fear. If we could only see others the way God the Creator sees them the world would be a much better place. My prayer is that this book will help you in overcoming the abuse and humiliation of anyone that is controlling or bullying you as I have faced in my life. It's time to stand up and declare who you are and learn to appropriate the courage and strength that dwells inside of you. Sometimes that involves asking for help from others and most importantly asking God for help in understanding how to deal with the issues of life that arise.

Acknowledgments

Besides Jesus Christ, the most wonderful person I've ever met and who has been my biggest support is my wife Steffani. She has enriched my life with her compassion and kindness like I've never seen in another human. She is selfless, caring, and an example of the unconditional love Jesus demonstrated while he walked the earth. Steff is a wife of noble character and is her husband's crown as Proverbs describes. If you've met her you know exactly what I mean – she makes me look good!

My sons, Zach, Tyler and Derek: I cherish each of you for how different you are, while at the same time you are so much alike in your character, integrity, and masculinity. You are strong and at the same time honest and loving. You make me so incredibly proud of all three of you. The talent and gifts you possess are a blessing to everyone who knows you. You have brought joy to your mother and me that we never knew existed.

My daughter in law Tayler: you have brought joy and laughter to our home that only the wife to our son Zach and sister to Tyler and Derek could have brought. We love what God is doing in your's and Zach's lives and are excited for His destiny for your future.

My father-in-law and mother-in-law, Warren and Ada, to you I say thank you for blessing me and allowing me to marry your beautiful daughter. I call you Mom and Dad, because I see you as my second parents. I don't believe there are more supportive in laws on the planet. We have called you over the years for prayer and not only did you pray, but you have been there to support us when we've needed you and were going through rough times. You have always prayed for us and have spoken positive affirmations over us and believed in us and our three boys. You spoke abundant life, health, favor, and prosperity into our lives that got us to where we are today. I love you both very much and never imagined I would have such an incredible relationship with my in laws.

All my friends, pastors and mentors: You know who you are. You are the best friends I could ever ask for, and I treasure our friendship. Thanks for your encouragement and influence over the years that chiseled off some of my rough edges. You made up ten times over for the friends I didn't have when I was young and bullied. Thanks for eating greasy food and the chocolate fountain with me and laughing about it. Thanks for guiding me through struggles and tough days when I needed someone to talk to.

My cousin Bob, you have sharpened me like iron sharpens iron. You were the one and only person when I was growing up who never teased me. You were my idol when I was a chubby kid, and my passion for the woods and hunting probably stems from you taking me with you when we used to visit the north woods of Wisconsin. I always look forward to our retreats and hunts together. Thanks for giving me a greater love and divine understanding for donuts!

My dad, who was the greatest role model any son could ever ask for. He was a southern gentleman, even though he was from Wisconsin. He had more integrity and character in his pinky finger than most men demonstrates in a lifetime. He taught me to fish and hunt, and to love my wife and children like a godly father and husband should. As a minister his entire life, he didn't just preach about the love of God; he showed it to everyone he met. He lived the life he preached about in the pulpit and never compromised. My dad was the first person that knew I was bullied as a kid and he didn't like it at all. Those were fighting words for him and though he displayed great love in and out of the pulpit, when you messed with his wife or children, his German temper flared with a vengeance. He was the one who put an end to the school bullying when I was a child. Because he stood up for me, he will always be my hero. What a reunion someday to see him again in heaven. A year before he passed away, I asked him to bless me and asked him if he wouldn't mind writing it down. I remember Jacob in the Bible asking for his father Isaac's blessing, so I asked him to do the same. My father spoke and wrote a blessing over me, which hangs in my home office today that I will forever cherish.

My mom, who made me and my brother and two sisters stand in a row when we were about 4, 5, 6, and 7 and learn four-part harmony while she played her southern gospel piano. This would have been about 1972 when that all began. That was back when we still had black and white television! All my love for music comes from you, along with the southern gospel influence. You taught me to fight and be tough and loved us like only a mother could. You fought for us like a mother hen protects her baby chicks. I got some of my fighting attitude from you and your feisty Irish nature, which I am so very proud of. I'm so grateful and thankful Almighty God miraculously healed you when you were diagnosed with cancer at 74 years old without medical treatment. He still has many things for you to do here on earth and I love when we talk and I hear the excitement in your voice of others being healed and delivered by your ministry. I found the letter you gave me when I first got started in my banking career and was experiencing stress and anxiety and Steffani called you for prayer. Your letter was a word from God that even now over twenty years later still rings in my ear like the bell of the little white chapel dad pastored in Wisconsin as we were growing up.

What others say about *Bullied to Blessed*

Bullied to Blessed is an invitation to each of us to choose the empowered, overcoming mind of Christ rather than a victimhood mentality in all areas of our lives. Weaving his personal journey together with faith building Scriptural Truths, Dave first personalizes the importance of intentionally keeping right thoughts and words before us then he makes the Biblical principles contained in the various aspects of his story accessible to the reader. This book will challenge you, encourage you and ultimately call you to live a richly blessed life."

Jonathan Wiggins
Senior Pastor Rez Church
Loveland, Colorado

Thanks to David Besch for this excellent book that gives testimony to the Great God that is able to rescue and protect and transform all of us and help us with the challenges of life. David and Steffani are tremendous blessing to so many and my prayer is that all men would read this book to be better men of God.

Jerry Swanson
Author and Former Colorado State President
Gideons International

From Bullied to Blessed presents readers with an uplifting true story and a challenge to live a life that fully embraces God and His goodness. Personally, I was blessed and energized by the book, and I warmly recommend it!

Andrew Albritton, PhD
Instructor
Computer Information Systems Dept.
Missouri State University

After reading the first few lines of 'Bullied to Blessed' I thought to myself, "How on earth did a boy who was called such terrible names turn into such a handsome hunk, marry a beautiful woman, become a successful business man and produce three magnificent sons?" I concluded that I must read this book!

I quickly saw that the way to victory for Dave had no short cuts, but that it came through hard work, faithful perseverance and obedience to the Word of God. This book carries an encouraging and practical 'how to' in overcoming obstacles and impossibilities. The process is character building and though not always easy, the reward of becoming who God created you to be, is immeasurable. Freedom and victory are found in these pages.

Ellie Hein
Missionary to Mozambique

Chapter One

The son of a preacher man

"For I know the plans I have for you, declares the LORD, plans to prosper you and not to harm you, plans to give you hope and a future." Jerimiah 29:11 (NIV)

It was 1977. "Hey fat boy" were the words I remember being called walking around the playground at recess. Never really feeling there was hope for me. I had maybe one or two friends or maybe they were just nerds like me that felt rejected. But God had different plans. I was that kid that was always picked last in sports because I just didn't look quite like an athlete. Very shy, chubby, and freckles was how I looked, and then I had to get glasses when I was about 13. That sure didn't help me look very GQ. When puberty kicked in with pimples that only made it worse. I think I actually remember being called *pizza face, four eyes,* and *fat boy* all in one sentence once. Ouch! That's gona leave a mark!

Our parents did the best they could being pastors in a small community in the cold farmlands of Wisconsin. It was a pretty strict upbringing for four children in the home of a Pentecostal minister. Our house was a large, old brick, two-story home that sat on three acres right outside town. We had an alfalfa field separating our lot from the forest where Dad, my brother Kevin, and I hunted. Some years, we cut down our own Christmas tree as the whitetail deer danced around. That part of being a kid was great.

There was also a great place to sled when the snow came. The window to the bedroom I shared with my brother Kevin frosted over in the winter, and the draft of the cold winter air seeped in as I lay there every night thinking about the next day at school. I constantly daydreamed about the life I hoped to have someday—one where I wasn't fat and unaccepted, but muscular and well-liked by everyone.

Dad was a native of the dairy state and we were always Green Bay Packer fans. It was the most popular religion in Wisconsin, then Lutheran. Mom was a southern gal from Alabama who cooked better than anyone in the country—as far as I was concerned. I ate everything on my plate. Now I'm not sure if I did it because I was so hungry, Mom made me, or I was just trying to drown my fears, anger, and hurts. She insisted that we eat everything on our plate, but I never complained especially with her homemade bisquits and gravy.

Dad took me hunting and fishing, but mostly life was about church and doing God's work. Our family went to the lake once in a while to my grandparents' cabin, but we always made sure there was a church service going on during summer camping trips. God forbid we miss church, find ourselves in a night club drinking, or worse yet, a roller rink and roll our way straight to hell especially if the rapture happened. It may sound rough, but at the time that's how I thought. Self-righteous legalism kills and steals your joy.

Living in the home of a Pentecostal preacher was not always easy, but overall, I had it pretty nice. I just didn't always see it that way at the time. I had loving parents, food on the table, and fond memories of Christmas and birthdays in our home. The faith in God that was instilled has grown into something I never expected to flourish. I never realized when Dad preached about the kingdom of God that it was actually here on earth.

I felt different growing up from others due to our denomination. Legalism steals so much joy from people, where everything is sin. I constantly felt condemned to hell, which was depressing at times and felt like bullying. Now, I look back and realize how much more dysfunctional and unhealthy so many others I knew had it. I understand abused children and abused mothers have it much worse, but at the time there were a lot of negative emotions related to living this way. I look back now and am so thankful for my heritage and the values woven into our moral fiber. I wouldn't trade any of my life with anyone I know and I wouldn't want to be anyone else. As a matter of fact, I like who I am today because of the ethical, moral, and loving upbringing we enjoyed.

Everything happens for a reason. Even in death, we see that God uses a person's life to help heal others. Through difficult times and circumstances, the best gift my parents ever gave was their unconditional demonstration of love and positive attitude. I observed my dad as a young minister being ridiculed and hurt by many. Nothing left a lifelong impression like seeing my dad hurt and crying. That's ingrained in me forever. He never wavered in his faith and courage though. He brushed off the hurt and never held a grudge. When I came to realize that I possessed the ability to change the course of my life, I could then begin to enjoy inner peace and joy the scriptures talk about as being Kingdom Living.

I made a choice somewhere along this journey to change my thinking and attitude, and begin to see myself as a winner. I went from a chubby kid being picked on and bullied every day to realizing I was a child of the most-high king, and that I was made in the image and likeness of my Creator. Because of that understanding, we can realize that our very soul comes from the actual breath of God Almighty. "And the LORD God formed man of the dust of the ground, and breathed into his nostrils the breath of life; and man became a living soul" Genesis 2:7 KJV. With all of God's creation,

He spoke it into existence, but we were the first and only of His creation that he actually used his hands to form!

When I determined in my life to stand up for myself and let my voice be heard, things begin to change. It's one thing to have positive thinking and affirmations, but you have to take actions. Your behavior needs to change. Now is the time to stop moping around in self-pity and stand up and be all that you can be. So many people say, "well, I'm trusting God will work this out for me". That's okay to say, but the scriptures say in Ephesians 3:20 (KJV) "Now unto him that is able to do exceeding abundantly above all that we ask or think, according to the power that *worketh in us*". So many people leave off that last part that says "worketh in us." Yeah, we are saved by grace, but if you want to experience abundant life, you must take action. You must quit blaming the devil for all your problems and blaming God for not answering when you are able to do so much more than you ever thought. It all starts in your head and your thought process. There are a lot of authors writing about thinking and positive thoughts, but why are they all writing about it? Because it works, that's why!

When you begin to believe in yourselves and realize you are capable of achieving anything you desire, you will see the course of life change for the better. You can live in victory and not always feel like you are a victim who never gets a break in life. There are sometimes physical and economic limitations to achieving some of your desires, but you can look deep inside and ask, "what are the dreams and desires I have in life? What is it that I want to achieve and fulfill?" When your motives are right and your desires line up with the word of God, they are achievable and your divine destiny to fulfill.

Day after day of being called names, pushed, bullied, punched, beat up, and threatened was torture. Every morning I felt sick to my stomach from the nerves and stress of wondering what would happen that day. When children are bullied their self-image and self-worth are programed to believe the worst in themselves. "I'm fat," "no one likes me," "I'll never get a girlfriend," and "I'll never make the football team." It goes on and on. Those negative thought patterns can actually make a person physically, emotionally, and mentally ill. Later in life I developed diverticulitis, which I directly attribute to my early childhood thoughts of negative self-worth. The good news is that I haven't suffered from that terrible disease in years and believe I am completely healed. People can be healed through prayer as the Bible talks about, but there are consequences that come directly from our own thinking and actions.

One night as the winter wind whistled through my window, I plotted revenge on a bully. How could I get him back without retaliation? Could I pay someone to beat him up for me? Maybe I should just end it all and get it over with. My thoughts worsened until I was envisioning some of the most evil ways of eliminating this one individual specifically. Except there was more than just one bully. Once others saw my vulnerability, they chimed in too. Our family was known as "the religious family" because we belonged to the Pentecostal church my dad pastored, so that made it hard when we weren't allowed to go to movies, dances, or parties like everyone else.

My introduction to bullying began when the boy sitting behind me in 6th grade music class started kicking my chair one day. I turned around and told him to stop. He then acted like he was going to hit me and said "Besch, you just wait until recess!" *Oh my word*, I thought! What would happen at recess? My heart raced and my mind went into a flurry of "what ifs". What if he beats me to a pulp? What if he breaks my nose? What if he breaks my arm? What if, What if, What if? We allow fear so often to paralyze us when over 90% of all fears never occur! Well, he pushed me around a lot and threatened me, but for the most part, he didn't physically hurt me that day. But that didn't mean there was not emotional pain, fear, and the feeling of constant harassment. When his friends saw my vulnerability and weakness, they quickly chimed in on the bully band wagon.

Another time a bully picked on me after school and my dad drove up to pick me and my siblings up. When dad saw what was happening, he took off in a dead sprint after the bully. Luckily for that bully, he had about a 50-yard head start or no telling what my dad would have done. That kid never bothered me from that day on, but the bullying never did seem to stop from others.

The bullying was an everyday event. I was called fathead, fat boy, and many other degrading and humiliating names. When you hear this constantly, you begin to believe it whether you realize it or not. For years I thought of myself as fat and a loser. By the time I became a teenager, the few friends I did have all had girlfriends, but I never did. Feelings of hurt and rejection can easily take root and later on in life cause problems–problems with relationships, health, and continued poor self-esteem. When you learn to identify the roots of pains deeply embedded in your very being, you can dismiss them and the consequences they bring with them. You have been given power to overcome the circumstances in your life and to experience positive self-image and confidence in yourself.

What's unfortunate is that so many people who have been bullied as children end up allowing others to bully them as adults as well. I've experienced this several times early in my career as a young banker. Managers with a chip on their shoulder or were going through something within themselves tried to humiliate me and make me feel less than. This happened on a regular basis until I stood up to them with boldness. When I say "stand up to them," I'm not saying to pick a fight with them. Human nature, especially in men with anger issues, wants to react in this manner. As a young man, I walked away from fights about 90% of the time. Most of the time because fear gripped me on the inside I walked away not wanting to get hurt or humiliated.

Today I'm saying you need to STOP seeing yourself as the victim and begin to see yourself as the overcomer. You have the image of God almighty. Your DNA is divine and you are powerful. You possess royal blood because your heavenly father is the king. God has a plan and a future for you. It's a good plan. It's a plan of strength and courage to overcome and stand up for yourself!

A Turning Point

Years later, as an adult married with three boys, I wept in the office of our new home we had just purchased on December 15th, the week before a major Colorado blizzard. I wept because I was so incredibly thankful to God for what he had given to me and my family. I'd enjoyed 18 years of marriage to a woman who exemplifies the woman of Proverbs 31 (NIV). My Steffani is a "wife of noble character and she is clothed with strength and dignity. She speaks with wisdom, and faithful instruction is on her tongue. Her children arise and call her husband also. Many women do noble things, but you surpass them all." I have three sons who are totally blessed and highly favored although they were only 7, 9, and 14 at the time. I already saw a great calling on their lives. A parent's ceiling of accomplishments should be their children's floor, and that's how I have always seen my three sons. That's how I think and speak over my three boys constantly. They will be greater, more successful, and more prosperous than their mom and me.

Through financial difficulties, job loss, starting off in a small apartment, then to a small mobile home, living with in-laws, to a small home that worked when we had only Zach and Steff was pregnant with Tyler. But when Derek came along, we knew we had grown out of that cute little house. Many young couples face adversity early in their marriage mostly due to lack of wisdom. God says you can ask for wisdom and He will give it to you generously. I began to do that, it did not come over night. I'm still learning. We are all constantly learning. If you think you've arrived, you need to think again.

My career went from waiting tables and working as a telemarketer, to a struggling real estate agent, working side jobs, to 100% commission jobs as a mortgage broker again with more side jobs. I worked as a security guard during the nights and as a real estate agent in the day. I would be up all night and then go into the office, try to generate loan production and real estate transactions to make money. Finally the sleep deprivation and stress did me in. I experienced panic attacks and anxiety, which is rooted in fear. I remember the first time I experienced an anxiety attack. I woke up in the middle of the night and there was this feeling that something awful had just happened. It was like I was in the twilight zone. My mind raced with thoughts I couldn't even understand. One night it was so bad I called my dad in the middle of the night and the attack left immediately as he prayed over me. Thank God for a godly, spirit-filled father who knew how to make contact with God in the nick of time. I have heard of people committing suicide while having an anxiety attack. While I was going through this, my mother sent me this letter:

> "David,
>
> Immediately after Steff and I talked the other day, the Lord gave these words to me for you. My son, don't be troubled, for I have not given you the spirit of fear, But of power, and love, and a sound mind. And that sound mind is healthy, stable, solid mind, not tossed about with every wind of doctrine. I am your protection from all danger and distress. I am anointing you with fresh oil. I will instruct you in the way you should go, as you walk in my statutes and keep my commandments. Have I not said that I will keep you in perfect peace as you keep your mind

stayed on me? I will give you the desires of your heart because you have humbled yourself and sought me, thus says the Lord.

Love,
Mom"

Perfect peace were the words that rang in my ear and still do to this day. It is possible to have an inner peace even during difficult times. Declaring daily affirmations of positive life-changing words will change your future. I began to repeat these words daily my mom had spoken into my life and things began to change. I told myself, "I have perfect peace and I have not been given the spirit of fear but of a sound mind that is healthy, stable and powerful." Steffani spoke positive faith-filled words, too, and we began doing this with each other on a daily basis.

God spoke to Steffani one day and told her, "Tell David he is blessed every morning right before he walks out the door." The first time she did this, it felt awkward and strange. Soon after she began saying this to me, I landed a new job that qualified us for our first home. As the years went by, we continued telling each other we were blessed, and year after year, I got promotions, raises, and bonuses that blessed us exponentially. They were unexpected and unexplainable. God wants to bless all of us, not just to get us ready for the wealth of heaven and walking on streets of gold, but to advance His Kingdom, and He is doing it today as he blesses His children and they walk in obedience in their giving to others. The works of darkness are being torn down, and God's army is moving forward. Bullies are being defeated and destinies are being fulfilled.

A Christmas Present in a Red Stocking

My sister Sandra was born January 19th 1965 and my mom told my dad, "Well, I was thinking it would be a boy." Not that she was disappointed in having a baby girl; it was just a feeling she had during her pregnancy. My sister Sandra is an angel, or at least that's was she has been trying to convince us of her entire life! My dad said, "don't worry honey I'll give you a boy for Christmas." Dad didn't know at the time he was a prophet. December 25th, 1965, eleven months later that same year, early Christmas morning in a hospital in Phoenix, Arizona, I was born and brought to my parents in a red stocking. This was probably the typical thing to do for babies born on Christmas Day at this particular hospital. Approximately a month and a half later, a beautiful baby girl was born in Denver, Colorado who would one day marry this Christmas baby. She was born to the proud parents of an excited young couple who would be godly parents that prayed for the destiny of their children. Over twenty years later, the two of us met, and our future journey together began.

In the fall of 1987, I was walking across the college campus of Evangel University in humid Missouri when I saw Ms. Universe. She was petite with long curly hair, and every male head turned when she walked by, including mine. Later I learned that her beauty was more than skin deep, and the real reason she was there was to meet me! Her friend had told her about me before she had got to campus that year, saying she knew we were sure to be a fit. I didn't find out until later her friend had told her this. God was definitely speaking through Steffani's friend. She just didn't know it at the time!

My brother Kevin and I enrolled in this college hoping to make the football team, which we both did, but as sophomores in college, there are other things we were thinking about besides classrooms and studies and even football. I was also thinking about female companionship. I happened to find it with the most beautiful girl on campus.

My brother Kevin and I were very close growing up. We had similar interests and loved to walk the railroad tracks by our home in Wisconsin to a fishing hole we frequented in the summer. We also loved football and music. We dreamt of having our own Christian rock band someday. We were into Stryper back then. In later years, we returned to our roots of gospel music and became involved with the Evangel University's gospel choir. He played football in high school. As the short fat kid who played the tuba in the school band, I wasn't quite football material. Then I grew almost five inches during my senior year in high school and somehow made the Evangel College football team without ever playing a down of football in high school. I was a late bloomer and had a heart full of anger that I released when on the field. Even though Evangel College was a Christian college, I wasn't always praising God out on the field. A few bad words came out of my mouth a time or two. I highly admired the president of the college and was glad he never found out. I was the typical, rebellious preacher's kid with a chip on my shoulder.

I went through most of my life with very low self-esteem, as many do. When Dad and Mom moved to Wisconsin to pioneer a church in a little town of less than a thousand people, we experienced culture shock. I was overweight and very defensive about it because of the hurt and rejection, and I tried to drown my hurt with food.

I would have never guessed the beautiful girl I couldn't stop thinking about was also brutally wounded and hurting inside like me because of bullies, for different reasons of course. There were roots of pain, guilt, and shame embedded in her that we had to work through together to enjoy a fulfilled marriage. The devil tried to take her life on a couple of occasions, once in a drowning accident when she was thirteen where she actually died and miraculously came back to life. Her praying parents knew how to touch Heaven. God had a plan for her and for me as well. Looking back we can truly see how God brought us together.

Years of hearing God's word from Christian parents, teachers, and pastors would seem like a solid foundation for a healthy marriage, especially with parents who were incredible role models and living fulfilled married lives for many years. That's not enough, though. The Word says to fight the good fight of faith. A man has to figure this out with God's direction, and that only comes through letting pride go and humbling yourselves to the Creator of the universe. When you learn to submit totally to His plan and put your complete trust in His will, you can then come to the understanding of Kingdom Living here on earth, which means being totally ravished with your wife, healthy, favored and prosperous with peace and joy. My hope is that this book will encourage you to stay the course in your marriage, life, job, or whatever even if you feel like quitting. Don't be a quitter. God doesn't bless quitters. The bullies of life can come in like a storm at times, but there's blessing when you remain diligent. My prayer is that this book will plant a positive seed in you to keep you focused on the incredible future God has planned out for your life.

With the current world situation in constant crisis from terrorist and economic woes, now is the time for God's kids to shine. As you humble yourself, the Word says He will lift you up. That happens without you having to self-promote yourself through social media. These communication channels can be tools bullies use, so be on guard. Everyone seems to love to post their opinion, but unfortunately, it sometimes gets hostile and abusive.

Look at this time and season as not just challenging, but training for what lies ahead. Scriptures say that someday you will help Him rule and reign and even judge angels. How would that ever happen if you didn't have some intense training? I often wondered in the past why wicked or even just non-believer type folks seem to be so blessed, while honest sincere Christians struggle in areas of finance, relationships, health, and life. Psalms 73:3-5 (NIV) says "For I envied the arrogant when I saw the prosperity of the wicked. They have no struggles; their bodies are healthy and strong. They are free from the burdens common to man." Further on in that chapter, verse 16 says, "When I tried to understand all this, it was oppressive to me till I entered the sanctuary of God; then I understood their final destiny." Verse 19 goes on to say, "How suddenly are they destroyed, completely swept away by terrors!" The arrogant and wicked have an appointed time of judgement, so don't fret and be discouraged. God will get the final say. You will end up on the top and not the bottom.

Much of this walk is downright living in wisdom. Christians often make bad decisions in life in the area of investing, spending, and taking care of themselves physically and mentally. It's no wonder that a negative, poverty mentality dictates their life. Some of this is the result of being bullied. We try and cover the hurt with worldly pleasures and often times spend beyond our means. As believers and with increased in wisdom, we are now catching on. We are stepping forward into the kingdom living lifestyle and we're seeing the wicked falling.

Disclaimer: Through this book you may observe some differences between what I'm teaching and your own theories of interpretations or doctrine. I don't claim to be an expert in Hebrew or Greek. I simply want to share what's worked for me and is still working for me, as well as others. If you're not experiencing breakthroughs in your own life, you might want to give it a shot. Individuals, ministers, pastors, and church denominations who think they have figured out the exact meaning of how we should accept the entire scripture grieves me. Read this book for yourself, ask the Holy Spirit to reveal it to you "personally", and watch as you enter into abundant life. Ask God to help you make the right decision through the course of your life. I'm not criticizing pastors or denominations; they have been an important influence in my life. My own dad, who pastored for years and other pastors in my own life have impacted me in many ways. At some point, you must seek God and desire to hear Him yourself and also come under the leadership of a minister or pastor teaching the entire Bible. Keep a positive attitude and allow God to open your heart to new possibilities of looking at the Christian life of abundance, receiving His blessing and kingdom living. There is a future hope for you and it is full of good blessings.

You must have your heart ready to receive them. God does not want you harmed. You are His child and His most valuable asset. He wants you to live in peace and joy and abundance without lack. Getting God's words from the Bible engrained in your very being can bring new life into your spirit soul and body. The Word of God is active and alive that we can weave into our physical, mental, moral and emotion fabric to bring blessing we would have never thought were possible.

> *"For the word of God is alive and active. Sharper than any double-edged sword, it penetrates even to dividing soul and spirit, joints and marrow; it judges the thoughts and attitudes of the heart." Hebrews 4:12 (NIV)*

Chapter Two
Ravished with Love

"Let her be as the loving hind and pleasant roe; let her breasts satisfy thee at all times; and be thou ravished always with her love." Proverbs 5:19 (KJV)

While attending college in Missouri, I met Steffani one evening while doing back hands springs on the lawn with some of the guy cheerleaders from our football team. Yeah, I could do a backflip *and* at the time I weighed about 240 *and* played defensive tackle. Maybe that impressed her! Probably not so much as my wonderful charm and charisma!

When I kissed her for the first time at that closed down drive-in theater, I honestly saw fireworks in my head. I thought to myself, *I've got to figure out a way to hold on to this one.* I knew she was the one even before the first kiss. Folks always say you'll know when you meet the right one, and I definitely knew. Unfortunately, because of my past, I feared rejection, but God knew better.

When I look back now at how much I lacked in the area of wisdom, it's frightening. I was selfish, lacked self-control, and never really thought before I spoke. Proverbs 29:20 says, "Seest thou a man that is hasty in his words? There is more hope of a fool than of him." (KJV) In another verse, "Do you see someone who speaks in haste? There is more hope for a fool than for them" Proverbs 18:13 (NIV) Well that was me – hot tempered, self-promoting and at the same time suffering from a major lack of self-confidence. Being belittled and humiliated through life can have some bad side effects because of the shame and hurt. Thankfully God's love restores us back to the place where He wants us. That's the redemptive power of the cross.

Ravished with Passion

You hear couples say all the time, "we have a good marriage" or "we're very happily married" and they probably do have a "good" marriage or they may be "happily" married. But is it possible there is more, even more than a great marriage? What about a marriage ravished with passion and desire for each other like the first time you kissed your would-be spouse? What about the first time you knew he or she was the one you wanted to spend the rest of your life with and how that felt? When you were away from them and couldn't stop thinking about them?

Sound familiar? Is there a recipe for a perfect marriage? Are there key ingredients to having not only peace in the home and good communication, but cosmic, out-of-this-world excitement while driving home from work knowing there's someone waiting for you who loves you like no one in the world and can't wait till you walk through the door? Did being bullied have an effect on the way I would love?

Obviously good communication is essential, but it goes beyond that. Honesty and being quick to forgive are absolutes to a great marriage. Honesty means being able to express to your spouse if they hurt you or you are carrying an offense to something they said or did. Being bullied made me always on the defense and not always pleasant to live with. Thankfully God granted me a patient and caring wife who brought these behaviors to my attention in a gentle and loving way. You must be quick to forgive and to ask for forgiveness, especially when you don't think you where the one in the wrong. This can be a very powerful tool in creating peace and long lasting trust in your marriage.

Honesty also encompasses the obvious in terms of being honest with finances and time. Having separate checkbooks may have a purpose in some cases, but you must be open to each other viewing your transactions whenever you're requested to, either online or in your checkbook register. Where you spend your money is also where you spend your time, and keeping that information from each other is asking for trouble. Also seek honesty in answering to the satisfaction of your spouse why you need to work late, what you do after work, who you hang around with, and your other activities are very important in your relationship.

Trust takes time to develop and even longer to regain if it has been breached. Demonstrating the right behaviors and sometimes needing to prove your self is necessary. People bullied often need constant validation, and this can create a dysfunctional culture in the home. The great news is that God's grace is sufficient in every situation, and He will get you through the process.

Although being quick to forgive does not always re-establish trust, it is the first step in getting you to your final destiny. Many times you need to learn to forgive the bullies in your life from the past and even the present issues you may be dealing with. Friend, learn to let it go and forgive them. Most of the time they don't realize what they are doing and many times they bully others because they are bullied themselves or have self-esteem and control issues. Surrender them to God and let Him take control over them. The best thing to do is kill them with kindness and be the bigger person by not succumbing to their intimidation tactics. Ask the Holy Spirit to reveal the strongholds in the situation and fight the good fight of faith and believe God will work it out for your best interest. Ask God for wisdom, protection and self-control.

Keys to a Blessed Marriage

Over the years, Steffani and I have implemented certain keys in our marriage that have proven to work and bring Kingdom Living: peace, joy, and righteousness in our marriage. These keys have also helped deal with bullies as adults. Often we don't even consider them bullies, but they are, and sometimes they need to be confronted.

Our process begins with praying together every day with absolutely no compromise. Even if one of us is out of town on business or ministry, we call and pray together. The scripture says if one can put a thousand to flight then two can put ten thousand to flight. I believe this is referring to putting the devil and his demonic forces to flight. The prayer of a husband and wife is one of the most powerful prayers in the universe. Matthew 18:19 says:

> *"Again, truly I tell you that if two of you on earth agree about anything they ask for, it will be done for them by my Father in heaven." (NIV)*

The statistic for divorce in our society is very high, but among couples who pray together every day, the divorce rate is drastically lower. There are several studies showing specific differences in that rate.[1] When couples are faced with adversity in their lives and marriage, prayer is absolutely necessary. Praying in the spirit together even brings it to another dimension. The scripture says that our weapons are not carnal or of flesh but spiritual, and must be dealt with in the spirit and in our mind. You must first correct the discipline of your thinking for this to work. You can experience abundant life in your marriage when you look for what is the best in

---

[1] http://drstoop.com/the-couple-that-prays-together/
http://www.mattmcwilliams.com/divorce-proof-marriage/
http://www.huffingtonpost.com/2010/08/11/couples-who-pray-together_n_679130.html

your spouse, learn to trust them, and learn to make their happiness the most important thing in your life.

After we became certified marriage counselors, Steffani and I counseled a couple who were several years older than us. They were having marriage problems, and we suggested they begin with praying together every day. That is pretty easy homework and a fairly simple takeaway from a counseling session. After two weeks we had another session with them and asked if they had been praying together. The man stated that they hadn't and he just didn't feel comfortable praying in front of his wife. Pride, anger, or fear were likely the prime reasons he felt this way. He may have had resentment towards his wife for some problem that he caused in the first place.

My response was real simple. I told him he was wasting our time and their time even returning for a third session. I asked him, "Why are we here if you didn't discipline yourself to do the very minimal step that works?" It's amazing to me as a man that in studying marriage problems, it seems that about 90% of struggling marriages are because the guy was just selfish, and fearful. When men can put their pride in their back pocket and grab their wife by the hand and pray a covering and blessing over them, it is amazing how God will show up in their marriage and shift things around. So many times we are waiting for God to step in and make everything right when we have to take the first action and step out in faith and declare good things in our marriage by praying together.

When men stand up and be the godly leader of the home that they have been called to be, their wife will respect their husband as they fight for their marriage in prayer. Women tend to feel secure and safe when they see their husband demonstrate godly characteristics. I challenge every husband to pray with their wife every day at a minimum, and more often when there is an attack or wisdom is needed. God says He will give generously more wisdom to those who ask.

Marriage Prayer

Sometimes when we have felt bullied in our life we act in fear. Praying together is not a reaction to fear, but communicating with God. When our powerful minds are keyed in on Almighty God being allowed to take control of our life, and as we discipline ourselves to make the right choices, we will see an abundance of joy and excitement in our marriage that many don't think possible. I have several best buddies I enjoy spending time with, but Steffani is my best friend in the entire world. We pray together, laugh together, and yes cry together. She is my biggest support and I am hers. She believes in me more than anyone I have ever met. I believe in her in the same way. One of our main goals in life is to still be holding hands into our 90s and enjoying each other the same as we do today.

Now, men, when I say pray together every day don't make that out to be harder than it really is. However, this doesn't mean just praying at the dinner table, although that can be a good start. If you don't know what to say, start off with the Lord's Prayer. Even if you think you know how to begin, this is probably the most perfect prayer you could pray. It focuses you on the Lord and His provision, and reduces your problems to the specks of sand they really are.

> *"Our Father which art in heaven, Hallowed be thy name. Thy kingdom come, Thy will be done in earth, as it is in heaven. Give us this day our daily bread. And forgive us our debts, as we forgive our debtors. And lead us not into temptation, but deliver us from evil: For thine is the kingdom, and the power, and the glory, forever. Amen." Matthew 6:9-13 (KJV)*

A typical prayer that I pray with Steffani every day may go something like this:

God we thank You for today and that Your will be done in our lives. Forgive us of our sins and shortcomings and help us not to have any bitterness, envy, strife, jealousy, fear, or anger. I cover (our family, by name) with the blood of Jesus.

We thank You for divine health, favor, wisdom, protection, and supernatural abundance in our finances. We surrender every aspect of our lives to You and Your Holy Spirit. We summon the angels of the Lord to watch over us and fight on our behalf, and we thank You that no weapon formed against us will prosper. We bless our parents with health, strength, and provision in their life, and ask You to protect them from any harm or danger.

We bless our church and our pastors with health and prosperity. Give them wisdom to lead, and protect them from those that would speak or come against them. Give them discernment when they need it and understanding to make the right decisions in every situation. We bless the missionaries we support (name them) with favor, provision, and protection, and we also bless Israel. Protect Your people there and give them grace and mercy to understand Your Son Jesus.

Thank You Lord for all Your blessing and for helping us to be good stewards of all You have entrusted us with in Jesus name, amen.

This prayer is a bit different every time and there are sometimes we will pray for specific issues we know about including family or friends dealing with crisis, illness, disease, financial difficulties, emotional hurt, etc.

There is no perfect prayer to fit every occasion, but maybe the above will help you and be a guideline for you to start your own. Regardless, learn to build scripture into your prayer and declare positive blessing in your life and watch what happens. It is powerful when you implement positive prayer and you see circumstances shift and change.

After Steffani and I finish praying, we always tell the other we love them and state "you are blessed." Then seal it with a kiss! Try this and see if something supernatural begins to happen in your marriage and life overall. The most powerful of prayers are when two (husband and wife) pray and believe together. I am ravished with my godly wife and you can be too!

God has a specific, divine plan and purpose for your life. He has it mapped out for you, but you must make the right decisions guided by prayer to follow that map. He has shown that to me more and more through the years. He will put the right people in your path—even the right spouse if you are not married.

The fact that my wife drowned and died when she was thirteen, but then was brought back to life through the power of her praying parents, demonstrated to me divine purpose in that we met and she was exactly who I needed in my life to help me overcome my inferiority complex and low self-esteem. The loving wife and blessing she has been to me has more than made up for the bullying I went through early in life. We were definitely made for each other. I am her number one fan and have encouraged her over the years, and she has impacted and continues to impact the lives of many people through her ministry. We both truly believe God brought us together, and our desire is to see the hurting, the captive, and the lost brought to salvation, healed, and set free. What great things we can accomplish when we walk in prayer and unity.

Chapter Three

What's your true value?

"Look at the birds of the air; they do not sow or reap or store away in barns, and yet your heavenly Father feeds them. Are you not much more valuable than they"
Matthew 6:26(NIV)

Holding a .22 pistol to my head with the hammer puller back as I considered suicide because of hurt, feelings of hopelessness, and rejection was not the way out. What was I thinking as a young man? Nothing is worse than considering taking your life and leaving those behind with the pain and anguish of your death. I've seen it too many times. Parents never get over that hurt as they feel responsible for that mistake made because of bullying. Yet I found myself in that position. I wanted to end it all. I can't imagine what my family would have gone through because of my decision. I put the gun down and began to weep. I remember crying out to God for help and saying, "Please take away this hurt and pain".

There's no bully, group of bullies or rejection out there that should drive us to that point, but it happens. Schools, social media, work places, relationships, and other pressures of life can feel like they have taken their toll. If those hurting people could only see the plan God has for their life down the road, they would never let that thought cross their mind. If I could have seen His plan I would have never even put that gun to my head. I look back now and can't believe I considered killing myself. There is so much to live for. God takes our sorrow and turns it to joy. He replaces the hurt and rejection with favor and acceptance. Friend, trust God is getting ready to turns the darkness into light. The darkest hour is just before dawn. He's going to bring you into a new season of hope, courage and blessing. Hang in there and watch God work on your behalf!

God took the hurt and pain I lived with and turned it into a life of joy, laughter, and peace with a beautiful wife, successful career, and four incredible children in my life. Today I feel so blessed sometimes I don't think it's even fair! Don't do it–don't pull that trigger. Put the gun down. Put that bottle of pills down! Get out of that running car in the garage. There's hope and there is a way out. God's plan for your life is one of fun, fulfillment, and hope. Don't let the thoughts the devil puts in your mind cause you to act upon them. There is hope. There is destiny. There is a wonderful life ahead. God is getting ready to prosper you and grant you divine health. Don't let that financial struggle or illness get the best of you. Hold your head up high and know you are a child of the King of kings! He has healing and financial blessing He's getting ready to pour out on you when your heart is right and you fully trust His word.

Too often we see ourselves as less than perfect and criticize how we look, how we act, or what we have accomplished in life because of what people think or say. You may think, "Well, I don't have a job like that" or "I don't make the same amount of money that my friend does". Others may say, "Well, I'm too fat", "I'm ugly" or "I'm too short". Negative thoughts and words like this can cause anyone to become depressed and discouraged. Continuing in this path of thinking is detrimental to your life and self-esteem. I struggled with this for years being a chubby kid and constantly teased. Even as an adult, I've lost jobs, didn't fulfill expectations, or just under-performed. These issues can make us feel less valued.

I eventually saw myself as a loser going nowhere in life and never really accomplishing anything. Young children are very vulnerable, and feelings of insecurity can damage their future as an adult. Close the doors to these thoughts and words and begin to lay negative and toxic thoughts like this at the cross of Christ and see him throwing them into the sea of forgetfulness in Jesus' name. Imagine in your mind that these thoughts are actual substances, dissolving into the sea. You are more than a conquer. You have God the creator living inside of you, which is the Holy Spirit. With Him living inside you, all things work together for your good.

Sometimes it may seem that you'll never get through this tough time in your life. But keep on holding on. God does not change. The scripture says He is the author and finisher of our faith, meaning what He sets out to do in your life is going to happen. When you yield yourself completely to Him, you will see His perfect will working before your very eyes.

Self-Image Influence

"Loan to Value" is a phrase used in the banking and finance industry. It's basically the amount of debt you have compared to the total real value of property. It really represents the equity in an asset. As a banker, my job was to consider the value of real estate versus the loan or mortgage owed on the property.

So here's my story: I was a fat kid who finally got in shape one day and then everything was alright.

Wrong!

I look at poor self-image as a high loan to value or the negative thoughts (debt) against your true value. When we learn to re-program our mind, or as the Bible states, to renew the spirit of our mind and see ourselves as Christ see us through his blood of forgiveness, our lives will improve. So much of what we think we should be is programed into us from media, magazines, TV, and

Hollywood. Instead, let the word of God determine who you are. The debt against you has been paid with the ultimate price on the cross. You are 100% free and no longer a slave to hurt, pain and poverty.

Here's some good news: Jesus paid your debt on the cross and made you perfect through His blood. You are valuable to Him. A low sense of value is not God's voice speaking to you. It is the enemy of your soul seeking to defeat you and get you down. You must recognize this and stand up within yourself and know that you can do all things through Christ that gives you strength. In God's sight you have been made perfect through the blood of His son. Hebrews 10:14 says: "For by one offering he hath perfected forever them that are sanctified." That's good news and a reason to live life to the fullest!

I grew up always wondering how could anyone be perfect. We are all sinners that need a savior and the truth is we can't in ourselves be perfect, but with what Christ did on the cross our father God sees us through the blood of his son as perfect!

Scripture states that the birds do not worry about how they are going to be taken care of, and we need not worry as we are more important than the birds of the air to our Heavenly Father. He will take care of us even when bullies are surrounding us.

I remember playing football one day in gym class, and the bully who constantly abused me lined up right in front of me. I remember the fear I had–and then as the ball was hiked, he slammed me to the ground as hard as he could. I tried to catch myself and landed on my pinky finger knocking it out of joint. To this day my left pinky is still crooked and is a reminder of what I went through as a child. It's also a reminder that I am an overcomer. I am strong in the Lord and the power of His might. I can overcome the obstacles that life throws at me and so can you! Let these words sink in and reprogram your thinking to start seeing yourself the way Father sees you.

It also reminds me it will never happen again. I became an

overcomer as the word of God says I am. I don't hold any grudge toward that kid. He may have had a father who bullied him or a big brother or uncle who caused him to be this way. Most of the time bullies are dealing with low self-esteem issues within themselves often times worse than the person they are bullying, The key to moving forward is don't hold a grudge. Forgive and let it go. Today I can honestly say I have no grudge toward anyone. What a great way to live. It is complete freedom and peace.

Stand up for yourself

The whole fat kid and getting bullied most of my child hood didn't stop once I became an adult. Employers often bully employees. I had this happen at one bank I worked. After I finally confronted the man, he lightened up. Did he change? No, but his behavior changed slightly such that I was able to tolerate him. He was a controller and an abuser, and was allowed to get away with this kind of behavior because everyone feared him, even the owners of the company. He injected a cultural poison into the company and created a toxic work atmosphere that left demoralized employees who felt unvalued. Low morale was created from just this one individual's behavior. Unfortunately the owners and others never understood how this affected employee performance and overall company production.

What I later found out was that he had a child who was stricken with a disease and another daughter who had a child out of wedlock. He was dealing with things that probably caused him shame, fear, or guilt. Was that an excuse to treat others poorly? Of course not, but if we know the underlying causes of the behavior, it can sometimes help us be sympathetic and try to give folks the benefit of the doubt. I found myself feeling sorry for the guy and praying for him and his family. He needed Christ to restore joy in his life. He just didn't realize it. He was too busy trying to make himself feel better by inflicting pain on others that he could not see how it was affecting himself.

Sometimes when bullies are confronted in the proper way, they finally see what they are doing and understand how that connects with their own feelings and experiences, and the behavior stops. In the example I gave above, the human resources department needed to step in, but they never took the appropriate actions, and unfortunately, the company struggled with low morale for a long time.

Digging up roots of pain planted early in life and confronting them can bring freedom. I challenge you to pray this:

> Anger, guilt, fear, shame, and rejection, I dismiss you and command you to leave the deep, dark recesses of my mind and heart. I release courage, contentment, confidence, and love in their place. I have inner peace within me. My mind is at peace, and I am calm and content. Any sickness, disease, or mental disorders that may have tried to form from these emotional stressors I cancel out in the name and by the blood of Jesus Christ.

When you repeat these affirmations daily and change your thinking, you will notice that the way you talk will change. You cannot go around saying, "I'm fat", "no one likes me", "I feel like I'm getting sick" or "well my dad had this disease" or "my parents were divorced and my marriage is struggling". No, you have to start speaking positive, faith-filled words that will alter your destiny. Say things like "I am in shape and I am getting into better shape", "I am favored with everyone I come in contact with", "I feel good today and I am walking in divine health".

God spoke the world into existence and we are made in His image, so we too can speak in the same manner and create our future. I have been accused of being a faith guy and even a name-it-and-claim-it man. I am guilty and admit it, but it's working for me and many others. This doesn't mean I don't get attacked once in a while, but when I do, I know I'm coming out of it. It's interesting because many of the same people who accuse me of this are "Debbie downers" and some live in constant sickness and poverty. They are also the very ones who say, "I always get whatever is going around", or, "if not for bad luck, I'd have no luck at all". What is that if it isn't name-it-and-claim-it on the negative side.

Most importantly reading the Bible and getting the Word of God on the inside of you will change your life and heal you from the inside out! Having a thankful heart, and worshiping, and praising God can help correct our attitude of doubt. Realize you have the DNA of the creator of the universe inside of you!

You were made in the image of Almighty God

Releasing judgment and criticism about yourself will allow you to heal from anger. Forgive yourself for your mistakes and hang-ups. We all have issues. The only perfect human was Jesus. Ecclesiastes 7:20 (ESV) says *"Surely there is not a righteous man on earth who does good and never sins,"* so come to the reality that we are all living in a fleshly body with desires that are not always righteous. The self-righteous legalist has a hard time with this. They don't realize it's not their flesh that gets saved, it's their spirit man. They're too busy worrying about their hair when it's their heart that's the issue.

Self-control, discipline, and willpower affirmations can help in this area. Say to yourself "I have discipline in my decisions" or, "I have self-control over my eating and my thinking patterns" Love yourself and all God has made you to be. You must love yourself to get ahead in life. We don't need to be arrogant or conceited, but we must love who God made us to be—because God doesn't make junk. You were made in the image of almighty God Yahweh Elohim who created all there is and was and will ever be. Repeat positive affirmations daily to yourself and remember whose image you were formed from.

Social media can create another form of bullying. I've seen young girls and boys alike use this as a tool to be cruel to others. Sometimes the course of action is simply to unfriend the offender. Maybe the abuser will grow up someday. If that doesn't work, consider changing your user "handle" and maintain it as a private account.

Unfortunately, bullies don't always grow up, or they may turn their attentions to someone else. Remember–you reap what you sow. Someday what you have done to others may come back to haunt you. The secular world calls it Karma, but followers of Christ know it as "reaping what you sow". They are similar concepts, but from different theological viewpoints. Reaping and sowing is a law of nature put in place by God. When you put a seed in the ground, it will produce something. A corn seed will produce a stalk of corn. The law of gravity operates similarly. What goes up must come down. We all have heard and understand these laws of nature but many times take them for granted. Understanding them and using them to our benefit can reverse evil generational curses in your life.

Start seeing yourself as valuable, because, Friend, God didn't make a mistake when He created you the way He did. There is a divine destiny and purpose for your life that only you can fulfill. Be all that you can be by believing in yourself and what Almighty God has created in you. You are made in the image and likeness of God, and that makes you significant.

> Genesis 1:27 – *"So God created man in his [own] image, in the image of God created he him; male and female created he them." (KJV)*

How could we ever believe we are not valuable with this truth?

If we are made in His image, we have His characteristics within us. We can create with the words of our mouth. We are beautiful. We are healers. We are full of love, joy, and peace. Trust in God's love to carry you through and to fulfill His divine purpose in your life. Believe you are valuable and worthy, and don't believe anything different.

Sometime we go through these trials to refine us and mold us into what God has planned for us in the future.

We can walk through the tough times and come out pure as gold. Like the three Hebrew children thrown into the fiery furnace, they did not even have one hair of their head singed from the fire. The Lord may know you have something coming up that may be tough, and this current trial is building your faith to get you through to the other side and make it across the bridge you can't yet see. Keep in mind that God Almighty is omnipotent, and He knows what the future looks like. He doesn't even live in time. Remember that when you are waiting for a prayer to be answered.

Isaiah 43:2 "When you walk through the fire, you will not be burned; the flames will not set you ablaze."(NIV)

Christmas is my favorite time of the year. Steffani and I both enjoy the holiday season and being born on Christmas makes it extra special to me. One of my favorite things to do around Christmas is to watch old movies. My favorite one is "It's a Wonderful Life" starring James Stewart as George Bailey. He ran a savings and loan in a small town. When word got out that the savings and loan was in trouble because of some missing money, the townspeople tried to take all their money out. George decided his family would be better off without him, and tries to take his life by jumping off a bridge into freezing water. George did not even lose the money; it was his uncle who lost it while making a transaction at the bank. So many times we think it's the end of the world and we are not always to blame.

When Clarence his guardian angel shows up on the scene, George was still not convinced his life was worth saving, especially seeing that Clarence hadn't even earned his wings as an angel! George said he wished he had never been born, so Clarence made his wish come true and allowed George to see what life would have been like in Bedford Falls without him. So many things changed without George's influence: the town was named after and owned by a grumpy, old rich man who kept people living in shacks. Because George wasn't running the savings and loan, families didn't have the opportunity to own their own homes. George's wife never married and was an old maid; the town pharmacist poisoned a kid and was sent to prison. Had George been there, neither would have happened. The quiet, friendly town of Bedford Falls was now Pottersville, a roaring Las Vegas-type city with bright lights and clubs and violence throughout the entire town. George realized his life had value, and decided not to kill himself.

We hear so many times about young people who take their life due to pressures and trials that they encounter and fear they will never overcome. Even if what we're facing cannot be overcome easily, there is never a good excuse to take your life. We might never know how we impact the lives of others in a positive way, but when we put our faith and trust in God, He will see us though our difficult times, and we will end up better off than before if we could just be a little more patient.

So often we let our thoughts run wild and think of the worst possible outcome that could occur in a situation. The reality of it is we do have guardian angels! Psalms 91:11 states *"For he shall give his angels charge over thee, to keep thee in all thy ways" (KJV)*.

Nothing is worth taking your life over, my friend. God has a purpose and destiny for your life that is full of blessings and joy! George Bailey was always negative and disappointed that he never got the chance to leave Bedford Falls and see the world, but what he missed—and what we so often miss—is that we can experience the most wonderful life right where we are when we have the right attitude. If we continue to pursue the dreams and desires in our heart, we can make them into reality, and in the meantime, God may have some people that need our help. Don't get discouraged. Get rid of any toxic thinking of taking your life. God has a wonderful life for you to experience!

Chapter Four
Thought Patterns and Visualization

"Thorns and snares are in the way of the crooked;
whoever guards his soul will keep far from them."
Proverbs 22:5 (ESV)

When the Apostle Paul said "I wish above all that you would be in health and prosper," I don't think he meant that it was okay to sit around and eat Twinkies and potato chips all day and take vacations you can't afford. You need to have self-control and discipline in your behavior and thought patterns. This all starts with your brain and what you are thinking.

To overcome the bullies in our life, you must renew your thinking. One reason we do not ever feel like we're getting ahead in life is our imagination, which is a powerful force. The scripture speaks of thoughts and how they impact our life. What are you thinking of right now at this very second as your read these words? When you allow these evil and toxic thoughts to stay in your mind, there is a domino effect happening in your very health.

What are you exposing yourself to today and throughout the day?

The title scripture references your soul. Your soul involves your mind, will, and emotions. Your brain actually generates electricity and because it does, you can come to a greater understanding of how powerful your mind really is. As in training our physical bodies, the word of God commissions us to train our thought patterns, which in turn creates our own self-image. The Bible agrees with what science has found, or should I say, science agrees with the Bible. The scriptures say that "whatsoever a man thinketh, so is he." What do you think about yourself? If you're constantly thinking of yourself as fat, unattractive, skinny, too short, bald, ugly, or whatever, that self-image you have of yourself will determine how you act toward yourself and others. It will determine your inner peace or the inner conflict you face of not feeling up to certain worldly standards. Whose standard is that? Well, unfortunately, television and Hollywood have created this fantasy image of what we should all look like.

What words do you use resulting from your thoughts towards your spouse, children and friends? If you're married, the words and thoughts you have of your spouse will negatively or positively affect your relationship. Do you think your spouse is cheating on you? Do you think they don't look or act the way you think they should? So many men and women need to go back to the days of when they were dating and the feelings they had for each other to re-kindle their first love. I remember one pastor stated that when he counseled couples having marriage problems, he told them to go back to the back seat of the car! Remember what happened there? Passion and romance for each other was almost uncontrollable.

The scriptures talk about returning to our first love. Steffani and I have implemented date nights in our marriage where it's just us. We enjoy going out with other couples and the fellowship in that setting, but putting your smart phone aside and focusing on each other and what each of you may be facing is powerful and transforming in building a long lasting marriage.

On a date night, don't feel responsible for coming up with a solution to a problem your mate shares with you. Sometimes it's enough to simply say, "I'm sorry this is happening" or "I'm sorry that person is treating you wrong." One of the worst things you can do is psychoanalyze your spouse and try and fix him or her. Just listen, pray and come into unity with each other.

A simple prayer with positive words of encouragement can go a long way in building each other up. It doesn't have to be some long thought-out prayer so long as it comes directly from your heart. God honors these prayers, I think, more often than when we pray for long periods of time where we try and think of every possible thing to say to change the circumstance. I have noticed that sometimes the short, honest prayers that come directly from the heart get answered faster. Quoting scripture during our prayer releases the forces of angelic powers that go to war on your behalf. I have seen this work many times.

Everything you expose yourself to impacts your thinking and actions. What do you watch on TV? What books and magazines do you read? Are they aligned with the Word of God or are they dabbling into new age and occult principles? I have heard of individuals who have read certain books that were not in alignment with God's word and then develop a sickness or disease from what they were reading. Toxic reading can program your mind to think unhealthy thoughts.

The internet is another source of good and evil that we can make mistakes in what we allow the windows of our soul (eyes) to see. You must be on guard at all times as the enemy sets traps. Even when our intentions are righteous the adversary knows our weakness. He is the biggest bully in the universe and he has strategies through various means like television, internet, books, and music that deter us from reaching our destiny.

Surround yourself with the things of God and keep yourself busy with activities that advance the kingdom of Heaven. When we submit our life to God in this way, scripture says we can resist the devil and he must flee. Keeping your conscience clear of evil, lust, and worldly desires builds your faith and trust so that you know life will be good even when you face tough times. Build a fence around yourself and your family with ministry, non-profit, or outreach activities that keep you busy advancing His kingdom.

Even the proper hobbies can help guard our soul. For years, my life was engulfed with bodybuilding and fitness. I ate, drank, and slept bodybuilding. I finally realized, however, that it became first in my life and was filled with lust and selfishness. That's not to say you shouldn't work out and stay in shape, but there needs to be balance in life. I was often grumpy because my diet deprived me of fun foods. One day Steffani said to me "you need to just go eat a bowl of ice cream and be happy!" I actually took her up on it and have been much happier ever since!

My conscience was always concerned about making sure I worked out every day and ate the right foods. A couple of times I competed in bodybuilding and between the diet, exercise, and obsession, I couldn't think straight most of the time. I had a one-track mind. Part of this was because of feelings stemming from my childhood of not wanting to be fat. Being overweight seemed to attract bullies. Unfortunately, avoidance tactics can become such a stronghold in that we lose faith in the rest of the world and even in what God has intended for us. Even though I have trophies for doing well in the sport, my obsession came between me and God's ultimate divine purpose. It wasn't all bad as I learned how to stay focused and visualized myself and what I wanted to be and look like. I went from playing college football hitting a weight of over 260 pounds to competing in all natural bodybuilding competitions weighing 179 with 4% body fat.

If we could only focus on what God may have for us and not our worldly and lustful desires, imagine where that could take us in life. How could our lives be transformed? When our thought patterns remain on godly desires and overcoming the bullies of life and not holding bitterness in our heart, we experience ultimate freedom in life. We all react differently to obstacles that come our way, but through daily prayer, meditation, and a thankful heart, we can enjoy this journey of life at a much greater level!

> "Cling to your faith in Christ, and keep your conscience clear. For some people have deliberately violated their consciences; as a result, their faith has been shipwrecked." 1 Timothy 1:19 (NLT)

Let it go!

Toxic thoughts can be triggered by circumstances and situations, past issues, or people we have had to deal with. You may have been beat up on the playground or by a gang. You may have been sexually or emotionally abused. But Friend, God's grace and power can help you overcome those past wounds so you can move forward with life abundantly and release the past and forgive those that have hurt you.

> "Instead, let the Spirit renew your thoughts and attitudes." Ephesians 4:23 (NLT)

The most powerful man or woman in the world is the one who can forgive the one who hurt them. That's true strength! Let go of the past and don't let it cloud your mind and thoughts. Don't let this unforgiveness rob you from the freedom and inner calm God desires that you experience. You can bench press 500 pounds, but if you have anger or bitterness in your heart, how strong are you really?

The word of God says to take captive these thoughts. This is something we must develop and train ourselves to do. It doesn't just happen overnight. I wasn't bullied as a kid and then when I was eighteen decided that was enough and everything was better.

Be patient and stay focused. You must persevere and endure, as this will develop your character into a stronger person.

> *"And endurance develops strength of character, and character strengthens our confident hope of salvation."*
> *Romans 5:4 (NLT)*

Dr. Caroline Leaf [2] is a pathologist who has studied the brain and demonstrated that thoughts are "real physical things" [3]. They look like trees with branches and take form based upon whatever our thought life consists of. If these thoughts are toxic and negative, then these trees, which are proteins and enzymes, look dead and wilted. If our thoughts are positive and of a biblical nature, they will be like a blossomed tree. The can change shape however, depending on your thoughts.

These proteins are the building blocks of our innermost being. How do you want to build yourself image? It must be with positive thinking.

> *"If anyone does not abide in me he is thrown away **like a branch and withers**; and the branches are gathered, thrown into the fire, and burned."* John 15:6 (ESV)

With God all things are possible. The scriptures are full of references to our ability to achieve much more than what we think we can. If you believe something and conceive it, you can receive it. Imagine yourself achieving the desires God has placed in your heart, whether that be owning your own home, driving a reliable vehicle, getting a degree, becoming a doctor, or even entering politics to help

---

[2] Dr Caroline. Leaf, 2013, Switch on Your Brain, The Key to Peak Happiness, Thinking and Health, Baker Books

[3] Dr Caroline. Leaf, 2013, Switch on Your Brain, The Key to Peak Happiness, Thinking and Health, Baker Books

change our nation. Even at the tower of Babel God recognized that the people of that day understood this doctrine.

Genesis 11:6 says " ... *nothing imagined they can do will be impossible for them.*" (AMP)

Ultimately what the people in Babel were attempting was to build a tower to Heaven, which was not in the plan of God. They built a large tower and were headed in that direction. There has been so much written, lectured, and preached about the power of positive thinking over the years because it's biblical. Even if you choose not to believe or accept this, it doesn't change the outcome. Even if someone believes something and it doesn't come to pass, it doesn't mean this law of positive thinking doesn't work.

There are times we want "things" that are not in the plan of God or are not the best God has for us. The scripture says, "*so my ways are higher than your ways and my thoughts are higher than your thoughts*"(NLT). The word also says that sometimes our prayers are hindered because of issues in our life. Some of these issues can include not honoring our spouse. There are many married couples today who do not honor each other and who harbor anger toward each other. This can hinder prayers and desires being fulfilled. Release and renounce the anger and see what happens. You'll experience freedom and blessings.

The key is staying in His word so that your desires are of a biblical nature and align with His word. Then you will see your imagination and desires fulfilled. Even if you are physically ill, crippled, or disabled, God's word spoken over your life will allow you to receive healing in your bodies and experience His miraculous power. God does not find pleasure in your pain. The devil comes to kill, steal, and destroy. Quit blaming God and start fighting the devil.

You might wonder how you can accomplish that. With the word

of God, we can overcome the biggest bully around. Read it aloud, quote it in your prayers, and memorize it with repetition so that it gets down in your very innermost being to change you! Doctors have seen DNA change in people who change their thoughts and way of believing[4]. You are more than just a mere human! You are created in the image and likeness of Almighty God and have been given the keys to release healing, blessing, long life, and abundance in your life. Start believing this and imagine what it will be like to be prosperous, happy and healthy!

I've always been a daydreamer, and over the years, I have used this to my benefit. Now I refer to it as visualization, which you can turn into reality. Even though I gave up being grumpy with the diet of egg whites, tuna from the can, protein shakes, chicken breast, and salads, I still do my best to stay in shape and eat right. Scripture tells us that our bodies are the temple of the Holy Spirit. Maybe we all need to do a little renovation on our temple! While I was into this season of bodybuilding, I visualized myself lifting a certain amount of weights for a certain number of repetitions. I visualized what I wanted to be and what I would look like. Remember, however, faith without works is dead, and you can visualize all day long, but unless you get up and take action, it will never happen. The scriptures tell us that we can renew our thinking and when we do we can prove God's will for our life and it will begin to manifest. Change the negative thoughts, desires and dreams to positive thoughts of health, prosperity and blessing others.

> "Do not conform to the pattern of this world, but be transformed by the renewing of your mind. Then you will be able to test and approve what God's will is--his good, pleasing and perfect will" Romans 12:2 (NIV)

---

[4] http://www.tribulation-now.org/you-dna-must-be-born-again/
http://www.charismamag.com/spirit/supernatural/27655-what-happens-to-your-dna-when-holy-spirit-and-your-human-spirit-merge

If you want to be the manager of your department someday – start seeing yourself in that role. Imagine what it feels like to obtain the wisdom and favor to be promoted. Then take the next step and train yourself in the areas you may not quite understand in that role. Bullies may come along and try to defeat and discourage you, but don't let them. Use God's word and be disciplined and diligent in your pursuit. Ask for projects to work on. Show the boss you want to go above and beyond your current role. Perform with excellence and be a person of integrity in terms of getting to work on time and even early. Don't be afraid to stay late once in a while. Going home and watching a crazy sitcom never earned anybody a promotion or a raise.

If you want to be a politician, you're going to need lots of prayer. We need good people in politics with biblical morals and values. Begin locally with your school district or city council and run for those offices to gain insight into the parliamentary procedures, and stick with your beliefs and values even when everyone else is different. God will honor this.

Not everyone can play basketball in the NBA or football in the NFL, so no matter how much we might want that, it won't happen for everybody. However, when God puts a strong desire in your heart to do something, don't second-guess yourself. Through the power of visualization, you can achieve and become more than you would have ever imagined. Picture in your mind what you want to achieve and to become. See yourself blessing others for the glory of God. See yourself being a person of influence, happy, healthy, and successful. Renounce the negative thoughts of worry, poverty, and sickness, and begin to enjoy this ride of life with positive thoughts of loving yourself and others. When you start by loving yourself and who God made you to be, it will be much easier to see yourself in a positive manner overcoming the obstacles of life.

Chapter Five
Word Patterns and Affirmations

"From the fruit of their lips, people enjoy good things, but the unfaithful have an appetite for violence."
Proverbs 13:2 (NIV)

Keep the enemy out of your life and far away with daily positive affirmations. You enter a covenant with God or with the adversary with the words you say. The scriptures say to give no place to the devil. The way we do that is with negative or evil words that we speak over our own lives.

Most of the time we do this unintentionally and don't realize it. We may speak words over our health, finances, spouse, children, or others. Sometimes we allow bullies to rule our life when we accept what they are doing and state words of affirmation about their action. We need to do the opposite and make statements such as "he/she can no longer treat me this way" or "I will stand up for myself." These words of affirmation must become a habit to speak and to believe in our heart. We then can take action through faith in our belief.

"He who guards his lips guards his soul but he who speaks rashly will come to ruin" Have you ever noticed that people who are quick to speak without thinking usually get themselves into more trouble than those who stay silent? At times, you must speak up and then

at other times, you should remain silent and let God act on your behalf. Thinking before we speak is a skill set that can be learned and mastered, but it takes discipline.

"When words are many sin is not absent, but he who holds his tongue is wise" Proverbs 13:3(NIV)

Many times when people talk a lot, they are trying to hide their guilt. Small children do this often and it can easily reveal their wrongdoing. Teenagers are famous for doing this as well. If they've been doing something they shouldn't, they tend to ramble on! Pay close attention and you can observe adults that do this, too. There's a reason God gave us two ears and one mouth.

Let me warn you—BE AWARE! It's not that difficult to observe someone who talks a lot and wonder what is going on in their heart. They try to cover their sins with many words. I usually avoid these types of folks as much as possible because of the toxicity they tend to spread.

When confronting bullies, sometimes the shortest statements are the most powerful. For example, if a bully criticizes you at work, you stating that you do not agree or do not identify with them will sometimes make them stop and think. However, if they have a controlling attitude or are abusive, be sure not to phrase these statements as accusations. Simply make a statement of fact, such as, "I don't agree with that" rather than "what you just said is wrong". Always act out of love and ask yourself "is this using wisdom if I say this?"

"The mouth of the righteous is a fountain of life, but the mouth of the wicked conceals violence" Proverbs 10:11(NIV)

When children of God impart good, kind, and gentle words

into the lives of others, it brings encouragement that lightens their heart. We need to keep this in mind to avoid gossip, always striving to bless others with our words, including the words we speak over ourselves. My wife utilizes this wisdom when she counsels women and youth. She is kind-hearted and always looks to encourage those who are upset or discouraged. She has been the greatest source of encouragement in my life. God knew exactly who I needed to marry to get me where He was taking me. She is always telling me how great I am and how blessed I am. She has done this with our three sons, as well, over the years. When I went back to school to get my master's degree, I was stressed. Steffani always spoke positive faith-filled words into my life that helped me get through. Be an encourager with your words. It will come back to you and bless you as God will place others in your life to speak positive, faith-filled words into your life.

Jesus said that we would do even greater things than He did. We must use the power He gave us. It is through the words we declare over our lives and the lives of others. So many times people keep praying and asking God for an answer when we have already been given the power to command things to happen in Jesus name. Speak it into existence and believe it in your heart.

If someone broke into your home and you were holding them until the police came, and then when the police got there and they said they needed to call the president to get authority to arrest them, you would think they were crazy. We tend to do the same thing with God. We ask Him for things when we have already been given the authority to command it in Jesus' name. We are sons and daughters of the Almighty Creator of the universe. As God created the universe with the words of His mouth, we too can create a positive, fulfilled life with the words we speak. The scripture states we can have whatever we want when we believe!

Speak to the mountain: " ... *have faith in God. For verily I say unto you, That whosoever shall say unto this mountain, Be thou removed, and be thou cast into the sea; and shall not doubt in his heart, but shall believe that those things which he saith shall come to pass; he shall have whatsoever he saith.*" Mark 11:22-23 (KJV)

Most men struggle with lust because we are visually stimulated beings. I hear men all the time say "Well, I struggle with lust" or "I just can't help it" Well, you sure can if you'd quit speaking that over yourself! Have some self-control and discipline. I heard a speaker once say, "We are all rotten sinners and need a savior". To some extent that may be true, but why keep calling yourself a rotten sinner? I found myself saying that over the years and finally corrected my speech. I now declare I am the righteousness of God in Christ Jesus and I am made perfect because of Christ!

> "*For we all stumble in many ways. And if anyone does not stumble in what he says, he is a perfect man, able also to bridle his whole body. James 3:2(ESV)*

It takes a strong man not to look and to lust in their heart. Be the stronger man. They say 80-90% of men look at porn. I say be the 10-20% that doesn't look. Now that is a strong man! Speak with your mouth that you are strong in the Lord and the power of His might. He says we can defeat the temptations of life when we learn to put on the armor of God. We must guard our minds with the helmet of salvation. The devil puts doubt in our mind, and the helmet of salvation can give us the assurance in our heart that we are saved and can overcome the temptations we face in life.

Women have their issues, too. Their problems tend to lie in the areas of security and love, which is why many women get caught in a different kind of fantasy, romantic love fantasy. Movies and books play on that, and include sizzling hot sex scenes that cause women to fantasize about being with the hero. Ladies, let me tell you—that is just pornography and lust by a different name.

We can take control of our life through discipline and self-control because God has given us grace to do so. It's a choice. The devil sets traps, and we can choose to submit to him or to God. We must submit to God and resist the devil **and he will flee**.

Women also struggle in the areas of jealousy and envy which can be major toxic thinking in their life. This can affect friendships, marriages, and even mental, physical, and emotional health. This behavior creates strife and hurt, even if their words don't specifically say so—it comes through in their words without them realizing it. Let it go ladies! Start confessing words to encourage each other instead of tearing each other down.

Speaking of words, there has been some debate about whether women talk more than men. [5] According to some studies, women speak 13,000 more words a day than men. I'm sure there are some that would disagree, but no matter where we are or what we're talking about we should have a goal to keep the focus on positive topics. I have personally witnessed men who never shut up, so this argument of who talks more is irrelevant to some degree. At the end of the day we need to watch our words and make sure we are not wounding or spreading gossip and strife.

Some people, including myself, have struggled with over eating. Some are even addicted to food. Much of this is cause by lack of self-esteem. This can come from you saying one simple sentence–"I can't help myself" or "I'm addicted to chocolate" Stand up today and realize who you are and that God created you in His image. You are

---

[5] http://www.dailymail.co.uk/sciencetech/article-2281891/Women-really-talk-men-13-000-words-day-precise.html
http://www.dailymail.co.uk/sciencetech/article-2281891/Women-really-talk-men-13-000-words-day-precise.html

great and mighty. *Greater is He that is in you than he that is in the world.*" *I John 4:4(KJV)* God says in the scripture you are blessed and favored when you put your trust in the Lord. Take control of your life and be an overcomer. You can do it. You have the power that raised Christ from the dead in your body. That is more power than any nuclear reactor on the face of the planet.

Some studies suggest that diseases such as diabetes are rooted in lack of self-esteem and an abundance of self-hatred. What words are you speaking over your life that could be the cause of health issues? I challenge you to delete them from your vocabulary and let God take control of your life in this area. Say something like," I will not eat that second brownie" or "I will not have more ice cream".

Not only is my gorgeous wife the most compassionate person in the world, she also has mastered the art of making my mom's chocolate cream pie, which is my favorite desert. My mom actually got the recipe from my German grandmother, my dad's mom, but Mom put extra whipped cream or something on it to improve it. Steffani went a little further than even more whipped cream. A few years after she had created these classics masterpieces, she decided grating a chocolate bar on the top and putting melted chocolate on the crust might be pretty fancy. Not only was it fancy, it improved the already incredible explosion of flavor that had been passed down from my German heritage. And I would eat and eat until it was gone.

However, I have learned not to eat half of the pie, but eating a controlled portion that still allows me to enjoy this divine treat. I say to myself, "I will not eat this whole pie in Jesus name." I also say things like, "I am self-controlled and I have discipline."

What ever a man thinks he is, so is he and whatever we say to ourselves, we can become.

I've heard people say "I have a drinking problem" or "my dad was an alcoholic so I struggle too." In certain alcohol therapy groups the first thing they say is "I'm an alcoholic". I understand why they do that—to acknowledge the problem. But once you've said it, that's enough. Now, instead of repeating that condemnation, speak, "I have overcome drinking and am self-controlled today." Blessed is the man who does not condemn himself.

When people are bullied, they tend to seek out things that they feel will numb the pain. That can be with food, alcohol, or in the form of bitterness and hurt. All of these can be toxic and harmful to our physical bodies. We must learn to watch our vocabulary as negative words can open doors in our life through confession of bad habits which can destroy us.

Why do I say all of this about eating and drinking, and what does it have to do with your affirmation and words? Much of our bad self-image and negative thinking from being bullied causes some to turn to these toxic habits as a way to forget the pain. My friend, no amount of alcohol or chocolate will numb the pain that only God can heal. Don't allow yourself to be deceived into believing lies and falling into the traps that the enemy of our soul, the devil, lays for us. This is a new season for your life beginning right this very second and no other delays will stop you from moving to the next level of God's destiny!

Joy and peace are kingdom living that only come when we take complete control of our word patterns. What we dwell on in our mind will come out of our mouth, and that will direct our destiny. We must learn to take captive, as the Bible declares, the thoughts that are against the will of God for our life. Imagine in your mind that wrong toxic thoughts are dissolving as you remove them from your mind. Confess that they are dissolving and you are strong in the Lord and an overcomer.

I sat on the board of a non-profit for a number of years that helped low income single parent families with scholarships, housing, daycare, transportation, and counseling. It was interesting to watch over the years as these parents; mostly single mothers would get encouragement from their counselors and end up becoming very successful in life. They believed in themselves and created a new life for them and their children. Words spoken into their lives became their new reality.

Missing father figures are a huge problem in this country. Many young children who are bullied lack a healthy father figure. A strong father was critical in helping me to overcome bullies and learn to stand up for myself. Absent or abusive fathers can actually heighten the problem and create worse consequences as the child tries to solve the problem without the direction of the missing fatherly advice

"Listen, my son, to your father's instruction and do not forsake your mother's teaching." Proverbs 1:8(NIV)

Our heavenly father can step in when the earthly father has stepped out of the picture however. God fills the void that has been created. Faith-filled words from our Heavenly Father can break the strongholds that limit us. State something like "my Heavenly Father has given me the strength I need to overcome this battle" or "my Father watches over me and will protect me and give me wisdom." If you don't have an earthly father, seek out a godly man such as a relative, pastor, or teacher who can impart words of encouragement into your life.

When I was teased by others for being chubby, my cousin Bob would say "it's all muscle, Dave!" Just his simple statement of encouragement would make me feel more accepted even though I knew it wasn't true. Someone out there cares and believes in you, so start believing in yourself! What Bob didn't realize at the time was he was prophesying into my life because later I did have more muscle than fat. If you don't have a father figure, maybe there is a cousin Bob in your life or an uncle or aunt that you can allow to speak into your life. Don't be afraid to open up to relatives you trust because God can use them to prophesy great things into your future.

Steffani and I went through a marriage certification program and became marriage counselors at our church. As we counseled, my greatest observation was men are not the spiritual leaders in their homes in many cases. They didn't have a clue of what that even meant. God has called all men to lead in a godly manner to bring protection, love, and safety to their homes. The words they speak over their wife and children can be positive or detrimental to their future.

My father was a great example of this. He prayed every morning for his family, and as he got older, he prayed for every single child and grandchild and even his great-grandchildren. He spoke words over every one of us, and today our family all love God and are all working to become better Christians and better people who love others. His positive affirmations over us got us through some tough times, even going through his own death. He would say we were blessed and anointed and favored. What a legacy.

My brother and I were raised to be masculine men who take charge; warriors, conquerors and protectors. Dad spoke powerful words over us. He did this with my two sisters Sandra and Rhonda as well. He always believed the best in us and spoke positive affirmations over us. Both he and my mother did not allow us to wallow in self-pity, but raised us to believe we were overcomers and had a great future ahead. Will you stand up and fight, and leave the same influence and blessing to your family?

Fathers need to lead by example and be role models in the way they speak words over their wife. They say children get their image of God from their fathers. There's no wonder so many have rejected God when their own fathers have been abusive or neglectful to them. Major influences into the lives of fatherless children in today's society are all but godly. Children get their role models and imagery of fathers from movies, social media, television, and magazine. Even other men in schools and churches have dropped the ball by not demonstrating godly character in front of children that are not their own. Our highest calling in life as men is to be great fathers and husbands foremost, and to speak positive affirmations over our families. Careers can come and go, and in many cases, you are soon forgotten when you leave a job, but your family will be there forever.

Our ceiling of success and accomplishments spiritually, financially, and physically should be our children's floor. What I do and accomplish in life will be only a fraction of what my three sons, daughters-in-law, and their families will accomplish. Steffani and I are constantly speaking positive faith-filled words over Zachary, Tayler, Tyler, and Derek. I tell them all the time they are way ahead of their mom and dad. We have instilled in them they are favored, blessed, prosperous, and healthy. We tell them they are going to go far in life and be great in the kingdom of God. I don't say this in arrogance, and if my father were still alive today, he would agree with this statement, but I will accomplish and be more successful than my father. I will build upon what he set as a foundation and take it to greater heights to advance the kingdom of Almighty God. These are positive affirmations I would encourage you to speak over yourself and your family. Tell yourself every day when you wake up and throughout the day "I am blessed, I am favored, I am healthy, I am successful, I am wise, and I am talented." Watch this become reality in your life!

We need to teach our children to know God loves them no matter what. Parents need to take the time to just listen to their children. In many instances, that's all that is needed. A child wants to be heard. And as we listen closely, opportunities will open to impart wisdom in a gentle manner that they will receive and carry through life with blessings chasing them down and overtaking them. Speak positive affirmations over your children and spouse. We tell our three boys and our daughter-in-law all the time they are going to be blessed and successful in life, even more than their parents.

We also cannot neglect to be there physically, emotionally, and spiritually for our children. Parents can break the bad cycles and break the generational curse of our fathers and forefathers and others who have negatively influenced us and our children so this is not passed down to our future generations. Try saying a prayer like "I close the door to all evil that has come against my family from generational curses." These declarations will change the course of your family's life forever.

I decided a long time ago that Steffani and I were starting our own, new family tree! It was a tree of blessing and good fruit. Our tree would be filled with favor, health, anointing, and financial prosperity. You can do the same for your family. Now if you don't believe this, that is your choice to live like that. I prefer a positive mindset of health and prosperity over one of poverty, sickness, and discouragement.

Don't get me wrong, there are times we get hurt and discouraged. We just don't stay there very long. We stand up, brush off the hurt, and move forward! I have lost several jobs over my life for various reasons. Somewhere from downsizing and some from being fired or severanced. Yes, it was hard coming home and breaking the news to my family. Yes, it was hard the next day, getting up, going out looking for another job. But I didn't wallow in self-pity. Instead, I brushed off the disappointment, updated my resume, and went out and found a new job. God always provided.

Friend, when you pay your tithes and are doing your best to be faithful to God, He always comes through for you. In the midst of the storms of life, get up inside of yourself and say "I am an overcomer, I have courage. The same spirit that raised Christ from the dead is living inside of me and I cannot be defeated."

Family dinnertime is a great time to share with our children and hear them out. The problem is so many families in today's society do not even eat dinner together. Even at Thanksgiving, I've seen the men eat their dinner in front of the television while the women stay in the kitchen or dining room. I remember growing up and having family dinner together every night. Now you are lucky to see this happen once or twice a week.

Our family's goal is to have dinner together as often as we can. For most families, life has gotten too busy and patterns that tear down the healthy family structure have developed. God intended there to be more unity and relationship in our families. It's easy to blame school teachers, pastors, and relatives, but it all starts in the home with the core family of a godly father and mother and positive faith-filled words spoken into each other's lives.

Our imagination is critical to all of this in terms of words we speak about healthy family, overcoming bullies, and building strong relationships. We see something on television, social media, in books or magazines, and we think it is the norm and should be the way things are supposed to be.

My friend, our guideline and map to a greater life is only found in the Word of God. The Bible gives us direction like no other book. Even some Christian authors I have read seem to have a distorted doctrine of how life should be played out. When you read your Bible, ask the Holy Spirit to reveal secrets to you and make His words come alive in your heart. God always honors this prayer and He is faithful to do whatever His word says.

Declarations and Affirmation words

Our words are very powerful. In the beginning, God created the world and everything in it with His words. By speaking it out loud it came into being. His word says we are created in His image, and therefore we have been given the power and authority to create life or death, health or sickness in our words. Many folks have taken hold of the story of the burning bush when God spoke to Moses and said "I am, the I am". When we wake up in the morning and say "I am" tired or "I am" sick of this job, it's amazing that we will actually begin to feel tired and sick.

What we should do is wake up in the morning and say "I am"

healthy and "I am" energetic today. I have several affirmations I say every morning and it goes something like this:

> I am happy, I am healthy, I am wealthy, I am successful, I am wise, I am talented, I am favored, I am anointed, I am a great father and husband, I am full of joy and peace.

When you declare this over your life, you will see the tide change in your favor. This is God in you or the Holy Spirit living inside of you speaking and creating your destiny. Things will begin to work out for your best interest in regards to promotion, peace, and joy in your life like you never thought or imagined existed. Does that mean nothing bad will ever happen? Well, of course not, but we can learn to fight the good fight of faith as the word of God states and overcome the bullies of life. And in the good fight, we always win no matter the circumstances.

Self-Control & Will Power

> Proverbs 19:3 (NIV) says *"A man's own folly ruins his life, yet his heart rages against the Lord."*

People are always blaming God for circumstances in their life that have occurred due to their own actions and decisions they've made. They will even blame the adversary, Satan. The majority of the time it is neither God nor Satan causing our problems but what we say and do in life and the choices we make. If you smoke three packs of cigarettes a day, your chances of getting lung cancer are much greater than someone who doesn't. If you don't invest time into your wife and family, you will not get their time and respect back in return. It's the principle of sowing and reaping again.

Not feeling fulfilled? These are traps the devil sets to snare our soul. We must guard our words, hearts, and minds, and walk in the spirit and not the flesh. This is a constant battle we must fight using God's word.

I constantly quote scriptures in my mind and out loud to help in this battle. Most people don't wake up in the morning and say "well, I think I'll get drunk today and get in a car accident" or "I think I'll have an affair on my spouse." No, the devil sets traps to deceive us and we must stay alert in the fight against our soul. I recommend starting off the day in prayer and reading your Bible. That's not to say it deletes all the traps and snares of the enemy, but I would rather put on the armor of God before I go out and fight in this reckless and immoral world.

Psalms 5:3 (NIV) *"In the morning, LORD, you hear my voice; in the morning I lay my requests before you."*

Destructive Affairs

I have observed men and women alike who have had affairs. So many times, this started with words spoken to a man or woman besides their spouse. And while most people who start an affair believe they will be happier, I've never seen that. In fact, several people I know who engaged in adulterous affairs died at an early age.

Proverbs 7:27 (NIV) says about the adulterous woman: *"Her house is a highway to the grave, leading down to the chambers of death."* Earlier in that same chapter, it calls the man "simple" who was led astray by her, meaning he lacked wisdom, discipline, and prudent decision-making. It also says in verse 22 (NIV), *"All at once he followed her like an ox going to the slaughter, like a deer stepping into a noose till an arrow pierces his liver, like a bird darting into a snare, little knowing it will cost him his life."* Friend, watch out for this trap.

Proverbs 6: 27 (NIV) also states, *"Can a man scoop fire in his bosom and not be burned"*? I have seen men and women alike who are caught in affairs then lose their house, kids, money, reputation, and all the things they worked so hard for, leaving them with nothing. It's a choice and we must make wise choices. Don't let flirting words with someone other than your spouse come out of your lips. Don't fantasize about what intimacy with anyone other than your spouse would feel like and look like. Don't spend time alone with an unrelated member of the opposite sex. You are asking for trouble.

The Bible talks about cutting off what offends you. What I believe this is saying is to get rid of the obstacle completely from your life. Completely avoid situations that have danger signs in view. For example, talking to someone of the opposite sex about problems you're having with your spouse is opening a door to destruction. Going out to eat in an intimate setting with someone of the opposite sex is setting yourself up for disaster. Working late at the office with someone of the opposite sex is asking for trouble. Not sharing your phone call log, text log, and email password with your spouse invites suspicion and mistrust.

God definitely sheds grace and forgiveness but consequences can last a life time. To inherit the kingdom of God, we must avoid the distractions that life brings our way. Stay focused on the prize and God's ultimate plan for your life and you will see Him work on your behalf. From our youth to a mature age, we experience character building by making righteous choices in life. Bridling our tongue with the words we speak must become habit and a pattern. Speak positive faith-filled words constantly and be on guard.

Don't open the Door

Spiritual warfare has been declared on you, your marriage, and your family. Build prayer walls to cover your marriage with supernatural protection. Ask God to stop any opportunities and then command the evil demonic spirit of adultery, lust, and sexual immorality to be dismissed from your thoughts.

Guard who you spend time with and what you watch on television and the internet. Do not open the door to evil and expose you and your family to disaster. Close every door of evil and ask God to show you doors you may have opened that you didn't realize would bring destruction.

There are times we open doors or allow things in our life that we don't recognize. This is where we must pray and ask the Holy Spirit to reveal anything we have done that we were unaware of. This needn't be a full-blown affair. Sometime we allow thoughts, words, behaviors, or influence to release evil. And sometimes the struggle isn't within us—it's within the other person. We can innocently speak words or touch a member of the opposite sex and communicate something we never intended. For example, a pat on the arm could be construed as intimacy when you were simply being kind. We can cancel these consequences through prayer in the name of Jesus and applying the blood of Jesus in the situation. All the forces of hell cannot prevail against you when you use the blood of Jesus in your prayers.

Ask God to purify your heart, cleanse your hand, and renew the spirit of your mind so you can be a vessel of righteousness to help advance His Kingdom. Take thoughts captive; submit to God and resist the devil and the Word says he (the devil) WILL flee from you. Break the habits that put you in compromising situations. When you pray, command the doors that have been opened by words you have spoken—even doors you were unaware of—to be closed and sealed by the blood of Jesus.

Control Issues

Women often enter a relationship outside of marriage because of an absent husband or one who lacks spiritual leadership values or several other reasons. If men would step up and be the spiritual leader God commanded them to be, this problem would not be so common.

Marriage is not a commitment but a covenant which should never be broken. Often times, marriages fail due to bully husbands. These men have control issues because they were bullied. Likewise, women can have control issues for various reasons. So many times, there is a generational curse that needs to be broken by the name and blood of Jesus to get victory. I encourage you to start a new season in your life. Don't wait any longer. Experience the joy of Kingdom living. Friend you can break this curse from your life and your marriage by praying the blood of Jesus over both. Praying in the spirit summons angels to fight on your behalf. Trust me—there is something supernatural that happens in the spirit realm when you pray in the spirit.

Discipline in our life in the areas of eating, drinking, exercise, words, and thoughts are vital to a healthy spiritual, mental, and physical life. Getting an education and being disciplined in studying opens doors of opportunity. Exhibiting good morals, standards, and values strengthens our credibility and reputation. I knew one man who would have been more successful if he had been disciplined when his eyes wandered. Proverbs says look straight forward, not wandering.

Stay focused on what you have to do and avoid the distractions that are all around us. Character is doing what is right when no one is looking. Living with integrity will bring blessing in your life in the areas of prosperity and peace. Eternal rewards wait for those who practice being a person of good moral character and integrity. Abundant blessing await you my friend. Begin to walk in them NOW and don't wait any longer.

Chapter Six
Create a Blessed Life through actions

"If you remain in me and my words remain in you, ask whatever you wish, and it will be done for you."
John 15:7(NIV)

This is not just another attempt at a self-help book to aid people with self-esteem issues. That industry is saturated by authors trying to psychoanalyze people. There are many secular books which use Biblical principles to assist you in becoming a better person, yet never give an ounce of credit to the original author and creator of the universe Almighty God. They promise more success, healthier bodies and minds, better marriages or careers, but the difference I'm presenting is based upon scripture. It starts in the following two verses and says:

"I am the vine; you are the branches. If you remain in me and I in you, you will bear much fruit; apart from me you can do nothing. If you do not remain in me, you are like a branch that is thrown away and withers; such branches are picked up, thrown into the fire and burned." John15:5-6 (NIV)

Many self-help books make it all about us and give no credit to

God. You can achieve great success in life by being positive, staying focused and determined, but to truly feel fulfilled, God must be in the picture or there will be emptiness and a void in your life.

The Word of God is Alive

What the above scripture is simply saying is that we need to read the Bible daily and allow it to saturate our minds constantly. I want to be brainwashed with the word of God! Most people need their brain washed anyway! We allow toxic and destructive thoughts to cloud our way of thinking so much of which comes from living in a fallen world and lustful thinking. Sometimes we need the help of others for guidance when being bullied, but the journey starts with our own choice of thinking and believing.

Every decision we make needs to be answered with the Word of God. There are some direct answers in scripture to questions about life and actions we take today within our current culture, but then there are other issues that we may not realize can be detrimental to our home, life and family. Even things like which television programs should I watch or is this book, art or sculpture ok for me to have in my home. It may sound ridiculous, but these decisions can create an environment in our home that is not God friendly. We open doors sometime to dark places without even knowing what we are doing. I strongly urge you to be careful what you bring into your home and expose your family to. This is where we read the scriptures and ask God and the Holy Spirit to give us discernment. The Word of God can literally become alive in our home where the Holy Spirit can reveal the answers to all of life's issues.

Hebrews 4:12 (NIV) says *"For the word of God is alive and active. Sharper than any double-edged sword, it penetrates even to dividing soul and spirit, joints and marrow; it judges the thoughts and attitudes of the heart."* When we speak His Word into a situation or decision, it summons the host of angels to fight on our behalf.

When we learn to appropriate this in our life, we truly understand the power Almighty God has granted to us as His children. As we begin to realize we were made in His very likeness and image, and by His words, He created the universe; we can then learn to create with the words of our mouth.

The scripture says that God calleth those things which are not, as though they were. By accepting Christ and His blood, shed on the cross, we take on a new DNA, which grants us the keys to the Kingdom and the power to do the same. The difference to making this reality however is abiding in the vine and remaining in God's word. This makes the process sustainable versus just a simple quick fix that fades over time. Praying God's Word, such as saying things like "greater is He that is in me than he that is in the world" or "with God all things are possible", calls down all the power of God. All things are possible means nothing is left out.

I went from being a chubby kid who was bullied to believing I could play college football and become a competitive bodybuilder, which I did. I also believed I could be a successful businessman, and became the president of a bank at 39 years old. I believed I could find true love and a beautiful wife and family to spend the rest of my life with, and it is happening! You can manifest a better life when you believe in yourself and who God created you to be. You can make dreams become reality by believing and taking steps to achieve your deepest desires.

Take the right path in life by believing and not doubting in your ability to achieve the impossible. Sow the right seeds in life by making corrections to the choices you make. Your character and reputation depend on it.

The scriptures say we'll reap what we sow. Many times there are problems in our life in matters of health, job, relationships, and finances because of behaviors or specific actions we have taken in the past. Proverbs 19:3 (NIV) states that: *"A man's own folly ruins his life, yet his heart rages against the Lord."* We often blame God for the negative circumstances in our life. For example, if we harbor envy, bitterness, or grudge, we may experience bone problems or arthritis. [6] Medical science has proven that our attitudes and being optimistic can directly affect our physical health. Proverbs 14:30 (NIV) said the same thing thousands of years before: *"A heart at peace gives life to the body, but envy rots the bones."* I have heard of many instances where people have been healed of arthritis who weren't even prayed for, but they released the envy or bitterness out of their life and were set free. We need to shut the doors of strife and bitterness in our life to experience health in our bodies. Positive thinking can also help with recovering heart patients and those suffering other diseases to make the illness short-lived. Begin to empty the toxic thoughts now for a healthier life of peace, abundance and joy!

Choice, Choice, and Choice

Most of us have struggled with allowing our emotions to control the decisions we make, and to a certain degree that can be acceptable. However, we have to choose to take the right action, whether that is in standing up to someone for their inappropriate actions or laying down that piece of chocolate cake when your pants were too tight that morning.

God has given you the ability to control your emotions whether you feel like it or not. He made you with emotions, so it's not always bad to show emotions such as when a friend has lost a loved one or if one of your children breaks up with a girlfriend or boyfriend. However, we must recognize when our emotional response gets out of control and can possibly be affecting our health.

We must choose to think positive thoughts when negative thoughts come to mind. This is not something that happens

---

[6] http://www.health.harvard.edu/heart-health/optimism-and-your-health
http://www.health.harvard.edu/heart-health/optimism-and-your-health

overnight, but must be practiced daily in our lives until it becomes a habit. Positive thoughts will affect your future and your ability to change the course of your life by choosing to take the right path. When you read the Bible and memorize scripture, then making the right choices becomes easier. When we learn to make the word of God a part of our everyday life, it alters the future and creates opportunities that would not otherwise have been there.

The way you think comes from what you listen to, what you read, and the influences of others. What you watch on television can also impact you thoughts. So many people watch hours of television and then wonder why things aren't going well in their life. You ask them if they've ever read the Bible and they will say "I don't have time", but they know every sitcom that's on every night. To have a closer walk with the Lord, you absolutely cannot leave out spending time with him in prayer and His word. Sometimes there are times where we are forced through our emotions to draw close to God.

If you've ever lost a job, a spouse, a loved one or your home, you have experience emotional trauma. Pain, fear, and hurt will sometimes drop you to your knees in prayer for help, comfort, and direction. As painful as these times can be, consider them opportunities to gain a greater relationship with Father God. If you experience uncertainty in life or financial difficulties, wouldn't you ask God for help? I can't imagine why you would ever want to turn from Him, when He is trying to get you to turn to Him for guidance. There are seasons in life and sometimes we feel like we are going through the fiery furnace of trials, but rest assured God will bring you through the fire as pure gold. When we are refined through the fires of life and trials, we come through as pure gold to be used as a greater vessel of service for His Kingdom.

Stay Focused on the Lord

Often when we go through these trials, they bring temptations, including the temptation to sin or to stop trusting God. The devil wants this to happen. He wants you discouraged and feeling defeated. We can't wallow around in self-pity, feelings of rejection, or low self-esteem and expect good things to go our way. Stay the course, stay strong and fight through, and you will see the goodness of God take control of your life. There are circumstances and even consequences that come our way to defeat us, but stay focused on the Lord and see yourself the way He sees you. You have been bought with the price of His Son on the cross, which is the highest price anyone has ever paid in history for the purchase of anything.

God will make a way for you to escape or come through the fiery furnace like the three young Hebrew men. Even though they were thrown into the fire, they were not burnt, but the king looked in and saw someone like the Son of God walking around in the fire with them.

Always know that God is with you. Jesus will never let you down. Even when difficult situations come that we can't explain, remember, there is a purpose for everything in life. Friend, there are some things that are above our ways that we may never know, and you cannot go through life questioning God and allowing your faith to be dissolved. Maybe God is trying to show Himself through a sickness or disease, to demonstrate His divine healing. Maybe this affliction will cause someone else to come to the knowledge of the saving grace of Jesus when they see how strong you are as you go through difficulties. Spending your entire life wondering is not going to get you anywhere. The bottom line is we will experience troubles, but how we react will determine the outcome of our future.

"Dear friends, do not be surprised at the fiery ordeal that has come on you to test you, as though something

strange were happening to you.But rejoice inasmuch as you participate in the sufferings of Christ,so that you may be overjoyed when his glory is revealed." I Peter 4:12-13 (NIV)

Taking actions to manifest a blessed life means choosing to set your alarm clock earlier and go for a walk or jog to lose those twenty pounds you've been meaning to lose. Or maybe you need to lay off the ice cream before bed. Ouch! That one hurt me as I struggle with that one.

Other actions may mean agreeing with your spouse to go to that marriage conference or marriage counseling. It may also mean taking action like simply getting off the couch and spending time with your children or spouse where there's actual conversation, or limiting Facebook or texting to fifteen minutes a day.

We already know most of the action items we need to take—we simply haven't applied them. I've learned that for me, fried foods, sugars, and processed foods can be unhealthy, so I limit them in my diet. An action item when you face financial problems may be to get a second job or have a garage sell. Stop spending beyond your means. Many Americans get caught up in the lifestyle that we perceive we need and overextend ourselves financially. It's not the end of the world. Renounce and repent of the frivolous spending and ask for God's grace then do something about it. The key is choice–one of God's greatest gifts he has given mankind is the ability to choose. Take action today and experience the new season God has for your life.

What is it you really want to do in life? Start taking the steps to make it reality, even if it is a baby step. Don't let negative people influence you to stay in the status quo of life. My sister Rhonda has always had a heart for young children to receive godly care. She has done daycare in her home for a long time, and years ago God placed it in her heart to start a Christian daycare facility. She had never owned her own business and had no formal training on how to start a business, but with determination and stepping out in faith, today she and her husband have one of the most successful Christian daycares in their area. She has a waiting list of people who want to send their children to her. She has so much favor with the community and families of the children that attend her daycare that they are planning to expand into a second facility.

When we step out in faith and pursue the dreams and desires God has placed in our hearts, we will experience the most exciting adventure God has for us that will impact lives throughout eternity, which is exactly what Rhonda is doing! These young children are receiving world-class care with godly values being instilled into their lives. There's no telling what one of them will grow up to become and change the world all because of what they may have learned at Mimi's Day Care!

Chapter Seven
Quantum Physics

By faith we understand that the universe was formed at God's command, so that what is seen was not made out of what was visible. Hebrews11:3 (NIV)

The nearest star to earth is Alpha Centauri, which is about 4.3 light years away or approximately 25.6 trillion miles; more than 300,000 times the distance of the sun is to the earth. Traveling at the maximum speed of a space shuttle or 17,600 miles per hour, it would take you around 165,000 years to reach this star.[7]

What this means is that if the sun were the size of a typical 1/2-inch diameter marble, the distance from the sun to the Earth would be about four feet; the earth would be barely thicker than a sheet of paper; and the orbit of the Moon would be about a 1/4 inch in diameter. On this scale, the closest neighboring star is about 210 miles away. That's about the distance from Cleveland to Cincinnati.[8]

The speed of light travels at 186,000 miles per second which is 670,616,629 miles per hour, so if there was a way to travel at the speed of light, you could get to Alpha Centauri in about 4.3 years,

---

[7] Earth Sky November 2, 2012, http://earthsky.org/space/alpha-centauri-travel-time

[8] Nasa http://www.nasa.gov/centers/glenn/technology/warp/scales_prt.htm

but based on what we know of space travel, it's impossible to travel that fast. You would burn up and disintegrate.

You are a walking Power Plant

Science continues to confirm many of the principles of the Bible that many of us are not even aware of. The above scripture, for instance, talks about creating things we can see, from nothing. Quantum physics studies particles and matter that are microscopic including atoms, molecules, and the energy they create. Atoms are what make up matter, and they consist of electrons, protons, and neutrons. The electrons orbit around the nucleus of the atom and some scientists believe certain electrons travel at the speed of light!

Now consider this: there are approximately 7×10^{27} atoms in the human body[9]. That is 7 with 27 zeros behind it! That is referred to as energy and it all is inside of you. Do you understand that you are not just a mere human of only flesh and blood, but you are a walking power plant of energy that can create? We were made in the image of Almighty God and we are an amazing work of art. We possess power that we have no idea we possess. Talk about a walking nuclear power plant–that's sort of what you are.

I began to see myself like this a few years ago and it radically changed my life. This was not in an arrogant way at all, but recognizing that we have the DNA of God the creator of all that exists or ever will exist is mind blowing.

Friend, when you begin to realize you were beautifully and wonderfully made as the scripture states, you can then begin to control the outcome of your life through positive choices you make. Choices that demonstrate and prove that if you believe and conceive, you will RECEIVE! This is not new age stuff. Proverbs 23:7 (KJV) states that *"whatsoever a man thinketh ... so is he."* And *"let the weak*

---

[9] https://www.quora.com/How-many-atoms-are-in-the-average-human

say I am strong" Joel 3:10(KJV) is also a scripture that proves that what we say, can and will come to pass.

"For as he thinketh in his heart, so is he." Proverbs 23:7(KJV)

"Let the weak say, I am strong!" Joel 3:10(KJV)

Sometimes we must take a position of denying ourselves or our fleshly desires to manifest certain things in our lives, but with the above scriptures, is there any reason to doubt you have the ability built into you to do so? The result is you triumph over fears about your past, AND eliminate them completely so they never return. The bullies of life can be overcome and defeated. You may have a bully of fear or anxiety that you need to overcome or a bully of disease that you need healing from. You may have become defensive and distrusting of others. I understand - I did too.

Friend, nothing is too hard for God, and what He has deposited on the inside of you makes you a champion. You need to make an effort, however. If you take the first step, God will thrust you into your divine purpose and destiny.

Supernatural Genetic Beings

Because of what Christ did on the cross, we were granted the keys to the Kingdom. The scripture says *"whatever you bind on earth will be bound in heaven and whatever you loose on earth will be loosed in heaven," Matthew 18:16 (NIV)* meaning we have authority to change circumstances and repel the attacks of the adversary. Get ready and be willing to walk in complete victory. Even in the storms of life, you can have a positive attitude to change your environment.

There are opportunities all around us to work in the miraculous and see God's hand working. You can unlock the door to financial blessing in your life by declaring it. Simply say, "I unlock the door to financial blessing and provision to rain down on my life so that I can be financially free and prosperous." Major breakthrough is about to come into your life in this area, so get ready and live with expectancy.

Our genetic makeup is of heavenly origin, and no power that stands against you can have dominion in your life. You have a direct connection with the throne room and God has given you the power to create your future. You have the energy and desire within you; sometimes you just have to wake it up on the inside. God's divine nature dwells in your very core being, and you are genetically positioned to achieve anything you want. No bully, no fear, and no evil words spoken over you can prevail. It's time to partner with your Father and receive your inheritance. You are supernaturally empowered to obtain all that God has for you, and I promise you it's more than you can imagine.

It's time to relax and brush off the worry and fear you've allowed to control your life and attitude. When you get upset and harbor bitterness, jealousy, or strife, it takes a toll on your physical body in terms of health and relationships. Start practicing today and release the supernatural power inside you. Start declaring you can do all things through Christ and declare you are more than a conqueror. Tell yourself, "I have my Father's DNA and my genetic makeup is heavenly and I am not just a human being!" You have particles inside of you that move at the speed of light, creating energy that is beyond the comprehension of science. The very fact that God has contained so much power inside of our physical bodies should convince us that we can perform way beyond our limits.

Because of bullies, I have had so much fear to deal with in my life that I would literally tremble in certain situations. My heart raced and uncertainty dwelt inside me, causing anxiety and restlessness. There were times I would wake up in the middle of the night with a panic attack and feelings of terror that to this day I don't know how to explain that feeling. It was like I was in the twilight zone or something. I'm sure some of you have been there. It's almost like an out-of-body experience. You feel helpless, guilty, shameful, and powerless. All sorts of thoughts run through your mind as it races uncontrollably toward a mental breakdown.

I remember one specific instance when this happened. I called my dad in the middle of the night, and he prayed for me, and within minutes, the panic attack left. Friend, if you don't understand the power of prayer and praying in the spirit, let me assure you it works!

Responding with prayer in every situation is critical to success in this area. God promises we can have peace and joy in our lives, and panic attacks and anxiety are not in the equation. To this day, I still recite this verse in certain situations. *"For God hath not given us the spirit of fear; but of power, and of love, and of a sound mind."* II Timothy 1:7 (KJV)

Making godly declarations that are faith-filled and sponsored by the word of God will change things in your favor. You can have miracles delivered faster than express mail. In many cases, we have seen instant miracles happen in healing or even answers come from a phone call or email while we have been praying. God does not always deliver the answer when we want, but He's always on time. Sometimes it feels like you get to the end of your rope and can't climb any further, but if you hang on for just a little longer, you will see a breakthrough. I have often told people "don't give up a day before your miracle"

Quantum physics is about energy, and miracles require energy to move mountains. We just need to learn to speak to those mountains in our life to make them move. Our voice carries power and authority when we speak and call things forth in the name of Jesus. Demons begin to tremble at the very sound of the name of Jesus. Don't settle for second best or try to "cope" with trouble–command them to leave your life forever as you submit to God and they will flee.

You must take risk to operate in the supernatural

For the supernatural to work in your life, you cannot operate or live your life in fear. You must take risks and step out in faith. Many times in our church, after we pray for someone, we immediately ask them to check themselves or move a certain way they couldn't before. That's faith! *Faith without works is dead* the scripture says. We must test ourselves after we pray. Sometime folks will only sense a small portion of improvement. They may say, "Well it feels about 20% better". Then pray again and ask God for complete wellness and wholeness. Then it may get all the way up to 80% better. Don't be afraid to pray again. When we are persistent with God, just like the small child that keeps asking and asking the parent for something, sooner or later the parent makes it happen for the child. Keep the faith and don't ever, ever give up.

We must also ask with thanksgiving first. BEFORE Jesus raised Lazarus from the dead, he looked up to heaven and said "Thank You, Father, for hearing my prayer". AFTER he had given thanksgiving, Lazarus came forth and lived again. To walk in the supernatural, you must take a risk and pray with thanksgiving. If that bully starts in at you, thank God for shutting their mouths and summon the angels of the Lord to close their lips so they cannot speak against you or harm you.

My friend Charles told me a story of when his aunt was confronted by a thief who flashed a knife at her and asked for her money. She didn't know what to do so she just started screaming "the blood of Jesus, the blood of Jesus, the blood of Jesus." The man was so bewildered, he ran off.

Friend, you are supernatural and it's time to activate it in your life. Know the Word, know how to appropriate it in your life, and see the manifestation of His power at work in your life.

"For you formed my inward parts; you knitted me together in my mother's womb. I praise you, for I am fearfully and wonderfully made." Psalm 139:13-14 (ESV)

"By faith we understand that the universe was created by the word of God, so that what is seen was not made out of things that are visible" Hebrews 11:3 (ESV)

"For in Him we live and move and have our being; as even some of our own poets have said, "For we are indeed His offspring." Act17:28 (ESV)

It can be difficult at times when the circumstances surrounding us don't agree with what the Word of God tells us in terms of making things out of nothing. Our strong stand and not wavering in our faith cancels out the negativity in life.

My mother-in-law is one of the most faith-filled and determined individuals I've ever met. She grew up with adversity as her father was blind and her sister was disabled, and she was left to raise her niece even while she was a child herself. Later on, she was involved in an accident that left her blind in one eye. Over the years, she could have become bitter and angry with God, but even today, with some health struggles, she continues to fight and stay positive and think faith-filled thoughts. She has been an encouragement to me and so many others who know her. She can meet a stranger on the street and help them turn their life around and offer them hope and you would never guess for a second that she has a care in the world. She speaks positive affirmations over my family and me, and has done so ever since I have known her. Everyone who knows her loves her and are constantly encouraged by her faith when they are with her. We must learn to act this same way and quit always thinking about our problems, but focus on the positive side of life and helping others. Then God can do a work in our lives.

We must look beyond the seen realm and into the heavenly realm. There is a supernatural world out there in a different dimension that is within our grasp if we would only learn to stay in faith and never doubt. When we allow wrong influences that dictate our thinking, heaven's systems cannot be released in our lives.

Friend, you must get this through your head and into your heart that as a born-again believer, you are not of this world. We are visitors here with an eternal home that goes beyond human reasoning. We can access that powerful heavenly system called the Kingdom of God as we continue allowing our minds to be transformed as our words declare His goodness for our lives.

Chapter Eight

Bulls-eye Focus

"The LORD said, "Look! They are one people with the same language for all of them, and this is only the beginning of what they will do. Nothing that they have a mind to do will be impossible for them!" Genesis 11:6 (ISV)

This portion of scripture references the story of the tower of Babel when the entire population of the world spoke one language. The people of that time said amongst themselves that they would build this tower to reach the heavens. They made bricks of clay with tar to hold the bricks together and built this large structure in hopes of making a name for themselves and keeping their people together. This was not the plan God wanted so He changed all their language so they were confused and could not continue building because they could not communicate with each other.

The key point is in the last portion of the story where the Lord is speaking and stating that because their minds could conceive this building, it was not impossible. As a matter of fact, this particular translation states that *"Nothing that they have a mind to do will be impossible for them."* He is telling us that whatever we set our minds to do, we can do it. When we get focused on achieving something in life, it is absolutely achievable. God almighty lives inside you, and you were created with power to achieve the unattainable.

Harvest a Great Reward

A bulls-eyed focus is an interesting concept. I am a hunter, and every year I head up the mountain to hunt elk and deer with my three boys. Before the seasons starts we sight in our rifles to make sure they are shooting straight. We want to make sure our rifles are accurate because we don't want stray bullets being fired, and we also want a clean kill shot. We never want to see animals suffer and always aim for a quick harvest.

What an excitement there is when you harvest an animal to feed your family, but harvesting a large animal like an elk it is extremely exciting. I especially love to see my boys get an animal. When my oldest son Zach was twelve, he got his first elk, and I was more excited than the first time I shot one. What an adrenaline that only comes with that experience. It's a very proud moment as a father and then to be able to clean it and pack it out. That experience made Zach an avid and skilled hunter. He is the first one out of all of us to start preparing when the fall season rolls around and seems to have a special instinct of where to find animals in the woods. It's like that with him when we're fishing too. He seems to always know where the fish are hiding. He can catch twenty fish to my one fish. It's been pure joy to see him become a greater outdoorsman than his own father. It's a lot of work, but well worth it, and it brings a lot of joy to me and my sons when we're together in the outdoors. Once we have fully prepared for our hunt, in our minds, we are already "locked in" on our target. We walk through the woods so quietly we have come upon elk and deer without them seeing or hearing us. This creates the right situation for our objective to be fulfilled with a successful hunt. We just hope we see them before Zach does!

"The lazy do not roast any game, but the diligent feed on the riches of the hunt." Proverbs 12:27 (NIV)

With a bulls-eyed focus and our minds set on taking our shot in life, we can achieve anything and harvest a great reward. The spirit of God is telling you right now there is unlimited potential within you. When bullies come to taunt you, it is not just possible to take authority over them and stop their actions, but it is inevitable.

Sometimes this does require the help of others. If you're young and in school like I was, I finally put my pride in my back pocket and asked for help. It was my dad who first saw the signs of me being bullied and addressed the issue. But the first step is for you to decide to get help and believe it can stop. If there is not a father around ask your mother, a counselor, minister, teacher or friend. You may have an uncle or other relative that can step in and support you. The key is do not let fear stop you from getting help. Ask that there be no retaliation or consequence from sharing your issues and concerns.

If there is racism or prejudice the bully may need a lesson in respect towards multicultural and ethnic differences. Unfortunately some adults would not even know how to address this or explain tolerance and respect of others. Conflict resolution can be challenging as we all come from diverse backgrounds and different value systems. So much of the mistreatment is from misunderstanding or because someone does not look like us or dress like us. Politeness and respect for others must be taught to the bully and then monitored. Verbal, physical and cyber-bullying can be stopped when we approach it in a responsible manner. Support groups that are working towards bully prevention are proving to have an impact, but we must get involved as parents and lead by example.

You must take that first step of action, which calls for intervention from an adult. In my case, a particular individual who constantly taunted me stopped. My father went to the principal of the school and asked for immediate action from the leadership of the school.

He also asked that there be monitoring of no retaliation because the guilty child had been found out. That is very critical in dealing with this type of issue, especially for the safety and well-being of the victim. You need to confront the school or organization's leadership for immediate action, AND also require monitoring for any possible backlash.

When children are confronted with these bullying acts, in some cases, the bully may not even realize what they are doing. Other times (and most of the time), they do realize what they are doing. Many times, they themselves are being bullied and abused at home, and this is the way they validate themselves to feel better in the midst of their dysfunctions. Also, peer pressure can cause bullying when "clicks" are formed from individuals with similar interest. If you are in a group like this, stand up and be strong. Don't run with the crowd, but rather be a leader and stand out in the crowd and show you have back bone!

My friend, nothing you put your mind to is impossible! Believe in yourself and feel empowered. If your parents are not engaged in your life or brave enough to confront the issue, then find another trusted adult to step in. It may be a pastor or adult from church who is willing to step in and help. It could even be a friend at school, a BIG friend! A fellow peer in a work setting can also offer support and direction. If you can't find anyone, ask the Holy Spirit to bring someone into your life to help. Then thank God for the help.

When we offer thanksgiving to God and worship and praise Him, He acts on our behalf and changes the situation. Jehovah God Almighty is a God of action and does not sit around and watch His kids continually be tormented when we take the right steps and our heart is right. All through the Bible, God took action on behalf of the Children of Israel when they offered thanksgiving, worship, and praise.

Stay focused and step out with your faith in God, and He will protect you. Keep your heart right, walk away whenever possible from a physical fight, and never be afraid to tell anyone who bullies you to stop. Speak calmly and kindly since yelling and cursing will only throw more gas on their anger and attitude. Don't lose sight—stay focused and watch God work on your behalf.

Distraction and circumstances can easily cause us to lose sight of what lies ahead for our destiny. Our culture bombards us with so much toxicity and secular thinking it can be difficult to keep our eyes on the author and finisher of our faith, Christ Jesus. Keep the faith and don't let a root of bitterness take hold of your life, as this is destructive and can cause us to get off track to the road of blessing God has planned for you.

I recently witnessed my youngest son Derek shooting an elk. It was an adrenaline rush. He had practiced shooting beforehand, but had missed his shot at an elk early that first day. He even got a second chance a couple hours later and missed again. Well first off his gun wasn't firing properly and sometimes in life we are not personally firing right. We get distracted or have not armed ourself properly. However, Derek was persistent and we kept looking. We hunted until it was almost dark, when finally he had another chance. He was poised, relaxed, and this time had a gun that was firing correctly. He put the crosshairs right on that elk, and shot it with an instant kill shot. He was so excited, as was I. He stayed determined and never gave up. He now is like this with his musical talents. He is so persistent playing instruments. He taught himself to play the drums and now is an incredible drummer, along with a great vocalist and guitarist. Don't ever give up. God wants to bless you abundantly!

Don't ever lose sight and allow the circumstances to distract you. It's easy to get off track at times, but stay focused and keep your eye on the prize because God's got a great harvest of blessing coming your way.

Likewise when we stay focused on achieving our dreams and desires, they come into existence. I recall on several occasions when my boys have asked me for things, and I didn't grant it to them right away, but they were persistent. Whether it was them wanting a new toy, visiting an amusement park, or looking at cars to buy, because they were diligent and focused, I responded as a father who wanted to see them blessed. Father God will do the same. He wants to give you the desires of your heart and bring increase to your life.

This portion of scripture rings true for your life today!

> *"Not only so, but we also glory in our sufferings, because we know that suffering produces perseverance; Perseverance, character; and character, hope. And hope does not put us to shame, because God's love has been poured out into our hearts through the Holy Spirit, who has been given to us." Romans 5:3-5(NIV)*

Chapter Nine
Relax and Lighten Up!

"So then, banish anxiety from your heart and cast off the troubles of your body" Ecclesiastes 11:10 (NIV)

Inner calm is a sense of knowing that everything is going to be alright. In the midst of the bullies of life, we can have peace in our mind. Sometimes, to unlock the key to peace and serenity in our lives, we need to forgive someone or release bitterness. When we have something negative in our heart towards someone, it blocks the peace of God that we should be enjoying in life.

When we get our focus off the person who harmed us and onto God and his word, we can overcome the anxieties of life. When you stop thinking about that job you lost and how mean that boss was to work for, you can then experience the true peace of God. Allow God's word to saturate you and renew your thinking. Stay steady and trust God's word for your life and He will take care of the rest.

"You will keep in perfect peace him whose mind is steadfast, because he trusts in you" Isaiah 26:3 (NIV)

All of us want to feel validated. Most people want to be accepted by others and have a sense of purpose. So many times, unfortunately, we make this our goal in life. This can be detrimental to us as we will never be able to make everyone happy. When you conclude that not everyone is going to love and adore you, your life becomes more peaceful.

There are individuals who will not read this book or will stop reading it because I talk about positive thinking and positive words and attitudes while they are facing difficulties they can't seem to find solutions for. What they are saying is they don't believe God's word because His word is full of positive affirmations for our life.

We can accept his promises or reject them. They have worked for me and countless others, so why not take a chance. What do you have to lose?

As you learn to quit judging others and focus on a closer walk with God, you'll walk in a supernatural peace that many will never experience. The truth is there are even some "friends" who will enjoy seeing you disappointed and discouraged because it makes them feel good knowing they have one up on you. Let it go–they are not true friends and have wrong motives. God knows their heart and He will take care of them. God has new friends for you and a new season is just around the corner. He has a fresh anointing coming your way that involves prosperity and power. You first need to let go of hurts and pain others have caused and quit judging others.

Relentlessly prepare and then Pray in the Spirit

I have been in situations where I needed to give a presentation while working in the banking industry, and bullies criticized me or questioned me to the point where I didn't know how to answer. I didn't know which way to turn or how to respond, but seeking God's word, praying in the spirit, and positive affirmations beforehand brought positive results. I then made this a practice in my meetings and presentations.

When you relentlessly prepare for something and then pray in the spirit, you will see God unlock promises of favor and power in your life. He will also grant you divine wisdom to know the answers to hard questions. God's presence can be with you in the midst of difficult situations as you experience His supernatural peace.

The Key is Thanksgiving

Philippians 4:6-7 says *"Be anxious for nothing, but in everything by prayer and supplication, with thanksgiving, let your requests be made known to God; and the peace of God, which surpasses all understanding, will guard your hearts and minds through Christ Jesus" (NKJV).*

You might want to thank God for all He has done for you and given you when you pray. As this verse says, when we do that, we experience peace that surpasses all understanding. Those who are not grateful and do not have a thankful heart will struggle constantly with anxiety, which is rooted in fear. The scripture says that *perfect love cast out all fear.* Therefore, when we walk in love and thanksgiving, we can eliminate anxiety, worry, and stress in our life.

It's so easy to get caught up in the cares of this world, especially in the current society we live and work in. It seems to be all about whoever dies with the most toys, wins. Try settling in to some quiet worship music. Begin thanking God for all He has done in your life and be grateful for what you do have. Practice showing love and kindness to others through actions and not just words. When was the last time you cooked a meal for someone who just lost a loved one? Or brought cookies to your new neighbor?

Let your identity not be in what you have, but what you do for others. It's amazing how working as the hands and feet of Christ will give you more peace and fulfillment than all the new cars or expensive vacations. In addition, you are advancing the kingdom of God by giving and caring for others.

Putting your complete trust in God will require the right choices in your thinking. Trusting is simply believing in something or someone. We can believe God's word because it is completely infallible. Prophetically, archeologically, and historically, there is no other book on the planet that has withstood the test of time and been proven over and over from generation to generation. When something like the Bible has such an incredible track record, why would we choose to follow any other way? We don't have to try and figure out how it's all going to work out or why such and such happen. We can completely surrender in faith the situation to God. Lay your troubles at the throne of grace and leave them there.

I quote the following scripture on many occasions when I need to trust Him.

> *"Trust in the LORD with all your heart and lean not on your own understanding; in all your ways submit to him, and he will make your paths straight." Proverbs 3:5-6 (NIV)*

Making the choice to trust and follow does not require hard or painful effort on our part, but we must choose to turn it over to Him. Thank God in advance for His answers. Jesus modeled this even when he raised Lazarus from the dead. We read, *"So they took away the stone. Then Jesus looked up and said, "Father, I thank you that you have heard me." John 11:41(NIV)*

A thankful heart will raise the dead! Do you have dreams that have died because of failure or disappointment? Maybe someone has discouraged you from pursuing your desires or told you couldn't achieve them. It's time to speak life back into those dreams with a thankful heart. Our dreams and desires in life can be fulfilled when we are thankful. God will work it out and turn things around for our best interest. Ask God to help you and cast your cares upon Him for he truly does care for you.

Stand up, stick your chest out, and hold your shoulders high!

Most of us worry and stress about the future. What will we eat tomorrow? Will that bully come to school today? Maybe he or she will be sick and not come in today. What will I wear to work? Will I make my goal at work, and if I don't, will I get fired? Will my son or daughter drive safe when they get their driver's license? Will they marry the right person? Will we have enough money for all the bills or for Christmas? It goes on and on.

Then we also worry about the past or feeling shame for a mistake we made. We allow the past to haunt our lives so we cannot have healthy relationships with others. This affects our performance and productivity at work and in life. Maybe you had a criminal record, a divorce, or you were raped or had an abortion and can't seem to release the feelings of guilt and shame. I've known others who were molested or abused by a parent, family member, or relative as a child. These are bullies!

Let me encourage you to live for today. Live for this very second. Declare "I am going to feel good and love others right now no matter what happened in the past." I told one of my sons when he didn't pass his driver's exam the first time "circumstances in life are going to happen, even when it's your fault. The key is how will you respond? Don't wallow in self-pity. Stand up, stick your chest out, hold your shoulders high, and go out and pass that test the next time"

To experience the inner calm and peace God promises, we must live in the here and now and not worry or harbor bitterness, guilt, or shame about the past. We must not stress or have anxiety about tomorrow. So many people spend over half their time worrying and stressing about issues that are already in the past or haven't even happened.

Most of the things we are having anxiety over are in terms of future events that never occur anyway. Live right now, live in this very second, minute, hour, and day, and choose to be happy and peaceful.

If you can't seem to shake the stress and anxiety read God's word, listen to music, take a hot bath or try natural supplements like gaba and magnesium[10]. Listening to music and meditating on God and His Word can help relax you and bring inner calm. Sometimes exercising more and eating right will contribute to a better frame of mind. Not getting the proper exercise and eating junk food will cause you to feel bad about yourself and experience poor health. This is not God's plan for your life. Practice self-control and discipline in these areas to enjoy a more fulfilling life.

My son Tyler is the most disciplined person I have ever met. He is up before everyone and on his way to the gym to work out. He eats clean foods and is the first to go to bed every night. He looks amazing! He has very little body fat and is strong as an ox! He didn't get that way from not being disciplined. He has been diligent for years and it has paid off. Self-control and a disciplined life style will take you very far in life. As the book of Proverbs states: *"The soul of the sluggard craves and gets nothing, while the soul of the diligent is richly supplied." Proverbs 13:4(ESV).* Tyler would not look the way he does or have half the energy he has if he didn't have these disciplines in his life. I tell him constantly he will go far in life because of his discipline. All the while attending college he has been working a side job and still manages to make time to work out and get good grades. God doesn't bless laziness, but He does bless those who work hard and Tyler is a living example of a blessed young man wherever he goes.

If you can't drum up the energy to exercise get a friend to go

---

[10] About Education, Anne Marie Helmenstine, Ph.D., June 10, 2014 http://chemistry.about.com/od/biochemistry/a/How-Many-Atoms-Are-In-The-Human-Body.htm

with you. Don't be afraid to ask for help! Even though people who are being bullied can have low self-esteem, they sometimes can feel better about themselves when they engage in activity. Don't have too much pride to ask for help. Family, ministers, teachers, friends, and even law enforcement may be necessary when we need encouraging or someone to lean on for help. Whether it's a bullying situation, financial problems, or stress, God can use others to get us through those tough times and gain some motivation.

When Steffani and I first got out of college we lived with her parents. This was when I experience sleep deprivation and stress due to working multiple jobs. One time when I was having a panic attack, my father-in-law was there for me. Like the true compassionate father he is, he put his arm around me and said, "Son, it's going to be all right." He prayed until I got freedom and peace to come over me. He remains a pillar in my life even today as an example of reaching out to others. I consider him one of my best friends and an example of what a godly parent truly is. He's also fun to hunt with, although most of the time our hunting trips end early and we find ourselves at the Village Inn eating a breakfast skillet with pancakes! Allow God to use those in your life to lean on when your drive and ambition has shut down. He places other members of the body of Christ in our walk to get us to our ultimate destiny. Hang on, get your motivation back and run into your blessed life.

Chapter Ten

Don't covet -- most of the Time

"But covet earnestly the best gifts: and yet shew I unto you a more excellent way." 1 Corinthians 12:31 (KJV)

Victims of bullying often wish they were someone other than who they are. If they were the star quarterback or the homecoming queen then maybe they wouldn't experience the bullying. Trying or wishing to be someone else will not solve the problem. Bullies come in all shapes and sizes and all types of backgrounds. Social media has increased bullying in schools and in other areas of life that has actually pushed people to suicide, which is the extreme. We cannot let this continue. There must be intervention when we see signs of this happening. Life is not hopeless. There is a way out when you're feeling alone and afraid. The heavenly Father is waiting with arms wide open for you to run to him for comfort.

Bullies often are jealous of others or are bullied at home. This occurs in adults in their careers and interaction with other adults as well. Unfortunately, we see a lot of jealousy in the church, which causes destruction in men, women, youth, departments, and even among fellow ministers. The leadership of the church should lead by example and often do not realize what they are doing. I will cover this in greater depth in another chapter.

We often covet someone else's life because we think it would be better to be them than who we are. We allow ourselves entry into a fantasy world by imagining we are someone we really aren't. It's fine to have positive role models in life, but we must make sure we don't get caught up in a fantasy world that doesn't exist or isn't the best plan of God for our lives. Someone who is constantly fantasizing is setting themselves up for a trap leading to destruction and disappointment. There's a difference between positive thinking and visualization, and fantasizing, and you must recognize the difference.

"Those who work their land will have abundant food, but those who chase fantasies have no sense." Proverbs 12:11 (NIV)

Men who fantasize about other women or women who fantasize about other men they are not married to begin to believe if they were with someone other than their spouse, life would be better. Individuals who are bullied will often fantasize to escape the world of reality around them entering into a land of acceptance and validation in their mind.

Our imagination can be used for many productive things and is one of God's greatest gifts to mankind, but we must check our motives of the imagination. The scripture says: *"Now to him who is able to do immeasurably more than all we ask or imagine, according to his power that is at work within us" Ephesians 3:20 (NIV).* The key to this scripture which most people fail to grasp is the last line that says the *"power that worketh in us."* This all starts with the imagination.

We need to imagine that God is for us and not against us, and that we are coming through this difficult time and are going to be victorious. We need to let the past go, live in the present, and look forward to the incredible future God has for us. There is a difference between imagining being someone other than who we are and who the word of God says we are. Trusting in this will set a positive direction for our lives and others that may be involved.

"He who works his land will have abundant food, but the one who chases fantasies will have his fill of poverty." Proverbs 28:19 (NIV)

I'll repeat this several times–It's all about the choices we make and the consequences of our choices. You will reap what you sow, and you will experience results of your thought life.

Having a strong desire to increase in wisdom and knowledge are two of the best gifts to covet. When you ask God to grant these to you, He does. In every situation or decision you have to make, ask this simple question "is this using wisdom to go this direction or that direction?"

If you answer this question honestly, you will not make the wrong choice. If there is a question in your mind, don't do it. If you're not sure if you should send that email, then don't press send. If you're not sure if you should say that to your boss, spouse, child, or peer, then don't say it. Wrong decisions affect so many areas of our lives, including our marriage, our relationships, our career, and even health.

The devil will attack our mind and try to make us think we need to spout off to someone who has done us wrong or to share it with others. In my daily prayer, I ask that God would help bridle my tongue as I have put my foot in my mouth more than once in my life. Friend, this spreads strife and will lead you down a path to a life without peace and joy. The devil is strategic in his tactics and he observes us and knows our weakness. This is where we must continue to fight him with the scripture. Don't allow the enemy to defeat you and get the best of your life and steer you away from your destiny.

"Whoever guards his mouth preserves his life; he who opens wide his lips comes to ruin." Proverbs 13:3(ESV)

If you're going to Covet

The scriptures say in I Corinthians 12:31(KLV) *"But covet earnestly the best gifts: and yet shew I unto you a more excellent way."* It goes on to talk about those gifts which are wisdom, knowledge, healing, miracles, and so on. These gifts are free for all who long for them. You don't have to beg God or seek out a prophet to come and tell you something about them; they are yours. You have the miracle working power of God in you, you ARE a healer, you ARE a conqueror and you CAN overcome the obstacles life throws your way! Gifts are free and don't cost you anything, so accept them and walk in abundant life!

If you do not see wisdom operating in your life, ask God how to get more. When we ask, we then take that step of faith to see it fulfilled in our life. More and more you are hearing of ordinary folks praying for people and miracles happening. Yes, there are faith healers who are being used to help people, but God didn't say you had to be someone great to have your own television program, and have a fifteen-thousand-square-foot home or a fifty-million-dollar Leer jet. You only need a willing heart and to say yes to Him. God uses the ordinary to do the extraordinary!

God watches over His word to perform it

Replace any greed or jealousy with God's gifts to advance His kingdom. Visualize people coming out of wheelchairs, people being delivered from addictions, hearts being healed, and financial burdens being lifted. Become active in the schools and community to help prevent bullying. Get off that couch and start making a difference in the world. Be a game changer!

What we can see in our minds can come to reality when we put our faith and trust in Almighty God. He says that He is the rewarder of them that diligently seek Him. God's word does not lie, and the scripture says He watches over His word to perform it, meaning God is not going to allow anything He said to not happen. We can put our faith and trust completely in Him to perform all that He said. If we keep the right attitude and believe, we will see miracles, signs, and wonders happen in our life.

> *"Then the LORD said to me, "You have seen well, for I am watching over My word to perform it." Jeremiah 1:12 (ESV)*

Ask God for the gifts you desire, and He will grant them. He is ready to increase you in wisdom, in knowledge, and in miracles – just ask. He will open doors for you. Keep the right motive and let your intentions be pure and see it happen.

The scriptures say we have not because we ask not. The Lord is standing at the door waiting for you to knock, and He will answer your prayer. Don't compare yourself to someone else. Don't desire the life of someone else. What God has for your future could be way beyond that person you want to be like. Settle in your heart right now that there's no one else you would rather be because God made you unique to His purpose and plan.

Often if we could see the other side of the life of someone we covet to be like, we would never want it. Sometimes what we see on the surface is not what is underneath. I have known ministers who seem to have it all together yet are abusive to their wife and children. We see this in professional sports and entertainment all the time. The ones we put on a pedestal and look to as role models are sometimes the ones with the most difficulties. How unfortunate it is when we hear of our favorite athlete being arrested for drugs or criminal behaviors – and these are the heroes of our society?

Be happy and grateful for who you are. God has empowered you with strength to overcome every bully in your life. God has an appointed time to make everything work out according to His plan. We just need to lighten up a bit and rely on His timing and not ours. Keep the faith, take a deep breath, and relax – It's all working out in your favor.

Chapter Eleven

Bully Managers

"For God hath not given us the spirit of fear; but of power, and of love, and of a sound mind." 2 Timothy 1:7 (KJV)

Supervisors and managers who bully us as adults can make us feel as bad as when we were bullied as a child—or even worse, especially when it involves your career and credibility. This can wear on your already-low self-esteem and self-worth. Many times bosses will act out in a manner of bullying to humiliate and belittle their employees in hopes of making themselves look better within the organization. Sometimes the bully supervisor is dealing with his or her internal issue that go way beyond what we can even imagine. Often there are control issues, and these people of influence are abusive charmers.

As an employee, if you miss a deadline or make an error, a manager may come down on you so harshly and abrasively that you feel of no value. Perhaps that was the manager's intent, but what if it wasn't? What if they think if they treat you bad enough, you won't make that mistake again. Their motive doesn't change the outcome, however, because bullying is something that is recognized by the victim, not by the abuser.

If the behavior is confronted but still continues, get assistance from the Human Resource Department or other managers. Maybe you'll need to explore your other options and get out of that toxic environment. I've had to do this on a few occasions in my career. But don't be fooled—there are bullies in every organization, and they are always on the lookout for "fresh meat". If you don't learn to resolve and face these problems, you're probably going to encounter them again and again.

Stand your Ground

When you confront the bully, and the behavior doesn't change, it's simply another form of the same behavior, except now you might believe that the problem is in you and things will never change. This can lead to stress, anxiety, feelings of self-worthlessness, and depression, which can affect performance so that we are managed out of the company. Unfortunately, that simply feeds our existing feelings of worthlessness and shame.

Instead, we must remain positive, confront the bully, and stand our ground. If we've made a mistake, we must admit it, apologize, make corrections, and take responsibility for the error. When we don't take ownership, managers get angry. The best way to head off bullying behavior is to be quick to apologize and ask how we can make it right. This stops the bully in his tracks, because now he has no cause to be angry, and we've included him in the solution.

We must constantly search ourselves to be certain we aren't setting ourselves—or our children—up to be a victim, like the young boy I remember from school whose parents didn't have the money to buy him new clothes, so he came to school dressed in too-short pants and outdated glasses which easily made him a target.

God can and will give us wisdom in this area if we ask Him to reveal the cause of the bullying. This in turn will help us understand ourselves better and seek help. Understanding the underlying reason why people act as bullies can bring freedom.

Sometimes we need to become better educated in our field to overcome the criticisms we deal with. I remember a boss who attempted to bully me because he felt I didn't understand accounting. The truth was, I did understand it, but I wasn't a CPA, and there were several things I could do to sharpen my skills in the area of accounting. Years later in my career I decided to go back to school and get an MBA, which included a lot of accounting courses. As I went through the course I understood about 90% of everything I was learning, but needed clarification on about 10%. I focused on these areas and ended up with straight A's in all my accounting classes.

When I turned in my grades in to my immediate supervisor and showed him I had straight A's, I politely asked him to put all questions of my accounting skills to rest, which they were. I moved along in my career rapidly and God opened doors for me with major increases in pay and promotion, because I humbled myself and took the good criticisms and left out the bad. Shortly after I received my MBA, I got a call from another financial institution that offered me a position along with the largest increase in pay I ever received in my career. This gave me an excellent return on my MBA investment, launching me to the next level of my career. What a great advancement and blessing. Keep a good attitude and trust God and He will bring promotion.

Be Patient and Work Hard

Over the years, I have had success in being a problem solver and meeting tight deadlines by becoming creative, being productive, and improving my self-esteem. Patience in a hostile work environment is not always easy. Some people enjoy making life difficult for others.

God uses situations so that later on you shine. Daily prayer, affirmations, and hard work of maximizing our God-given gifts and talents will strengthen and sharpen you. Be patient—promotion is coming. You are victorious and your hard work and patience is paying off.

Sometimes we don't see it happening in the physical realm, but God is doing something in the unseen spirit world to carve a path of success for you. "No pain, no gain" is a phrase we've heard about weight lifting. When you stretch yourself, you will be able to bend and move farther and farther. Don't allow yourself to become too comfortable. God's got you there for a reason which will propel you to the next level.

Be Humble and Meek

Managers who bully sometimes are arranged as a training ground for the greater plan and future that will bring about abundance, greater wisdom, and understanding. We don't learn unless we make mistakes, and sometimes that comes with criticism from bully bosses we don't care for. Try to give them the benefit of the doubt as they may be feeling pressure from their superiors or clients who have put pressure on them. They also may be going through personal issues that are private and unknown.

Of course, this doesn't mean they should be allowed to continue. Behaviors that goes unconfronted will continue, so don't be afraid to confront in humbleness and with a meek spirit–yet with boldness. Ask God for wisdom in every situation and He will make your path straight.

It can be difficult and hard to deal with, but our correct response to bullies in the workplace can be the key to defusing them. You deserve respect just as they desire, and there are times they need to be reminded of this. We are not to live our life walking on eggshells and constantly feeling harassed. There are times where more drastic measures need to be taken, such as getting a new job. God can bring you into a job where you are valued and can contribute to meet you goals and objectives.

Unfortunately, the Human Resources Department is not always the answer. They aren't always well-trained to recognize signs of bullying, and they are even less prepared to deal with it. In fact, they can sometimes make it worse. A good rule of thumb is - make sure you don't burn bridges when you leave. Acting with integrity will always be rewarded by the Lord. Don't allow your emotions to get out of balance and affect your health. Stay strong in God's word, get plenty of rest, eat right, and exercise. Remain calm and don't stop quoting scripture and positive affirmations every day. Be gentle when you speak even when someone else is nasty in their tone of voice. Remaining calm can make a bully realize how out of line they really are and, in some cases, you may see a change of heart. Don't forget *"A gentle answer turns away wrath, but a harsh word stirs up anger." Proverbs 15:1(NIV)*

Many times it takes years before we see how God uses adversities to refine us and cause us to become who we are. He used Job in the Bible as a great example of this. Job lost most of his assets, all of his children, and was stricken with sickness, but God knew he could endure, and in the end his life was greater than it was before the trials. Job came out on top and that's exactly how you will come out! You were created to be a champion, but that doesn't come without some intense training and hurdles to jump over.

I understand there are times we want to throw in the towel and give up the fight. I can't even count the times I have felt this way. Like the Psalmist David did, however, we must encourage ourselves and get up on the inside knowing that better days lie ahead of us. Don't let bully bosses get the best of you. You are more than a conqueror and have the power inside of you to rise up and be the better person.

"But those who hope in the Lord will renew their strength. They will soar on wings like eagles; they will

run and not grow weary, they will walk and not be faint." Isaiah 40:31(NIV)

"I can do all things through Christ which strengtheneth me." Philippians 4:13(KJV)

Chapter Twelve

Bully Spouses

"There is neither Jew nor Gentile, neither slave nor free, nor is there male and female, for you are all one in Christ Jesus." Galatians3:28 (NIV)

Many men and women feel bullied by their spouse. The word of God says in Colossians 3:19 (ESV) *"Husbands, love your wives, and do not be harsh with them."* I hear men all the time talk about them being the "authority" in the home and everyone falls under their rule.

Well, there is some truth about being the authority, but it does not mean they are the dictator and their wife is the doormat. I have seen so many times men who verbally abuse their wives and then the wife realizes that is wrong and dysfunctional, and leaves to be a happier person.

There are men who are controlers and do not have any respect for their wives or their opinions. The Bible is clear in the above scripture that in Christ there is no respecter of persons and that we are all equal in His sight.

Take Authority over the Adversary

The whole authority issues that some abusive men love to quote really gives them the "authority" to be the godly man that they have been called to be and initiate daily prayer and covering over their wife and children. We are to use this "authority" over the adversary the devil and fight the spiritual battles that come against the lives in our family.

The "authority" God gives men is to stand up and be strong in the time of adversity, to overcome the obstacles Satan throws their way. Men have abused this and have taken it to the level of dominance over their wives. We see this often in cults and religions that embrace a legalistic and self-righteous culture.

Real masculinity is to serve your wife with love. Often the whole dominance issue can lead to abusive relationships that turn sour and even potentially fatal. When making decisions, men have often failed because they didn't listen to God's precious gift to them in the form of their wives. A pastor once told me that 80% of the time when the Holy Spirit speaks to you, it's through your wife, so listen! Jesus said to you husbands *"Husbands, love your wives, just as Christ loved the church and gave himself up for her" Ephesians 5:25(NIV)*

Heaven's gates are open wide, and God has many blessings for marriages when two can come in agreement and align themselves with the word of God. Bully spouses can be either gender. Men and women both can be control freaks in a relationship, and eventually this behavior takes its toll, and the abuser finds themselves alone. God desires unity in marriages and this only happens when both spouses align themselves with the word of the Living God. Respect, honor and devotion to one another are absolutely essential to have unity in your marriage.

Emotional, physical, and mental abuse can and does

ruin a marriage. Sometimes physical abuse results in serious consequences. Unfortunately, the abused spouse often remains silent, thinking this is the best there is or somehow they deserve it. The bully spouse doesn't think they are doing any wrong and will struggle to admit it. What the abuser sees as abuse is usually different than the one receiving the abuse. Godly counsel is highly recommended in this situation, and intervention is usually needed with physical abuse.

Emotional trauma from bully spouses can be the worst to deal with because they don't leave marks of proof and you still have to live together. Bullies at work or school don't go home with you except in your mind if you let them, but a bully spouse is challenging. Seeking God and gaining counsel are keys to turn this around. The emotional scars left from this take time to heal and may never be completely forgotten. However, God is the restorer of marriages and can heal the broken heart of a distraught marriage.

If there are threats and violence in your marriage, you don't need me or any counselor or psychologist to tell you to get immediate help. You might have to stay with family or friends or find a safe house for protection. Acknowledging this dysfunction is the first step in breaking free from the situation.

Bring new Life to your Marriage

Humiliation and jealousy are other forms of abuse from a bully spouse. No one is entitled to treat you in a manner where you are embarrassed in front of others, or enforces a possessive attitude toward you in front of others. Maybe this has been happening to you, and you weren't even aware of it. Please understand that this is not normal.

Maybe you constantly check on your spouse or manipulate

them. Perhaps you have a temper that flairs up frequently and you struggle to get it under control. It's not too late. God's grace can restore and bring new life to your marriage. Forgiveness is very possible, but the abuser needs deliverance and complete freedom so there is no re-occurrence. It's hard to forgive abusers when they keep repeating their behavior and have no real change.

There are more emotional and verbal bullies than we realize, and quite often we find them right in our back yard with church goers. They hide behind a mask at church, and then change their behavior at home becoming a different person.

Friend, if you find yourself in either of these situations, please seek help from God and others. Change will not come until you take the first step. The change must begin with you. I see men all the time focusing on their wife being submissive, when in reality if they were godly men and exhibited Christ-like love as they should, their wives would respect them for the position of spiritual authority and leadership. And wives, if you are on the receiving end of this kind of abuse, please seek help. This is not your fault. You don't deserve this treatment.

You are not trapped

Bully spouses will blame the other spouse and place shame upon them. With these feelings of guilt, the abused spouse feels trapped. God's best for you is to have a loving, caring, and fulfilled marriage in every area. You are not trapped. Set yourself free in Jesus name. Do not continue down this destructive path. God's word does not support abusive marriages under the guise of women should be submissive. If this is your way of thinking, get your head on straight—your doctrine is skewed. God doesn't want you in an abusive marriage, but that doesn't mean you get to run out the door as fast as you can unless physical harm is being inflicted. There is hope. God restores marriages all the time and can restore yours if both parties are willing and will seek help. His plan is for you to enjoy each other and to grow old together with abundant life. Begin to choose thoughts of a prosperous relationship with your spouse and begin speaking it into existence.

> *"In the same way, you husbands must give honor to your wives. Treat your wife with understanding as you live together. She may be weaker than you are, but she is your equal partner in God's gift of new life. Treat her as you should so your prayers will not be hindered." I Peter 3:7 (NLT)*

Make sure you catch the end of that scripture! Men, if you don't honor your wife and treat her as your "equal" partner in God's gift of new life, you can pray until you're blue in the face, but nothing will happen. Honoring your wife includes when you are with her, and when you aren't. Maybe you travel for business. And temptation is all around you. After all, who would know? Honor means honoring at all times. Integrity is doing the right thing when no one is watching, but realize this – God sees all and is there when you're alone in a hotel room or on a business trip.

Maybe you aren't getting that promotion you've been praying for or you haven't gotten that raise you've asked God for. Well, how are you treating your wife? Are you showing her honor or are you just a bully and control freak? Start honoring and respecting your wife and watch your prayers begin to be answered!

When you start honoring your wife as the scripture tell you to, change will come. Until then you may just be chasing your tail for a long time until you humble yourself and obey what the scriptures says. And for goodness sake stay away from sexual immorality and pornography. Proverbs 17:20 (NHEB) says *"One who has a perverse heart doesn't find prosperity, and one who has a deceitful tongue falls into trouble.*" If you find you're not making any progress in life financially you might want to check your heart and what you are exposing yourself to.

I heard one preacher say that he was the head, but his wife was the neck that turns the head! That's an interesting analogy.

Many times God has given divine revelation to our wives but we don't want to admit it and listen. We think it will make us look weak and less of a man. In reality, great blessings can be right around your corner if you would heed this one simple admonition and listen to your wife.

Likewise, wives must honor their husbands. We live in a society and time in history where women have been taught that it's okay to be critical and belittling of their husbands. This is a form of bullying. If you are demanding of your husband, raising your voice at him to do things for you and wait on you hand and foot, your prayers can be hindered as well. Men can help their wives, and they should, but your husband is not your slave. Marriages are constantly being torn apart with separations and divorce because of mis-treating each other. We live in a day and age where kindness and gentleness is not a value we teach.

With the rise of women's liberation, we have seen an increase of criticism towards men in society. Part of that is brought on by abusive men, but part of this is a disrespect that has risen up toward strong men who live with integrity according to biblical morals and values. Speaking and praying blessings over your husband will go much further than cursing him or criticizing him because you don't think he makes enough money.

God rewards us with blessing when we honor each other. Bully spouses can be either gender. Husbands and wives alike dishonor their spouse. If you want to experience kingdom living, which is peace and joy in life, start honoring each other and give proper respect to one another.

> *"However, each one of you also must love his wife as he loves himself, and his wife must respect her husband." Ephesians 5:33 (NIV)*

Chapter Thirteen

Bully Preachers

"And I will give you pastors according to mine heart, which shall feed you with knowledge and understanding." Jeremiah 3:15 (KJV)

I am so thankful for the anointed pastors and teachers I have had in my life, but the truth is there are ministers who are convincing and manipulative, which can sometimes make us feel bullied. This may come across in the way they constantly ask for your money or in their condemning message of salvation. Many denominations are self righteous and legalistic in their teaching and interpretations of the Bible such that no one can come close to living up to. I grew up in a denomination like this and always felt condemned and never good enough.

One thing to watch for is ministers who do nothing more than use their position to manipulate you into giving. They are selling the gospel rather than teaching it and leading people to Christ. Pray for these individuals when you recognize them and do not fall into their trap of supporting them financially. Remember: what you feed will grow and make sure you are planting financial seeds in good ground.

Don't get me wrong—there is a lot of productive and good work coming from Christian media, with many hearing the gospel for the first time. We must hold these ministers in prayer that they hear from the Holy Spirit and that their motives are right. There is a watered-down gospel being preached in many pulpits across the world and especially in America. Accountability is key, and pastors, teachers, prophets, and evangelists need to be held to a standard if they are going to get up and direct the body of Christ into salvation, Kingdom Living and reaching the lost.

When you hear something being taught or preached that doesn't set right with you, first check your Bible to see the context. Use a good concordance and a Bible history reference. Ask the Holy Spirit to reveal the truth to you. Even the best television minister can misspeak or make a mistake.

"There is not a righteous man on earth who does what is right and never sins." Ecclesiastes 7:20 (NIV)

Always hold your minister up in prayer. Surely we have all heard something coming from the pulpit that didn't quite feel right. Sometimes it's just the delivery style or method of that particular minister or pastor that made it come across in a manner that he didn't intent it to be. Other times a doctrine goes against a teaching we were brought up with. In that case, we need to examine what we were taught, by going back to the Bible. Then compare this new teaching with what God says in the Bible. There are often times new teaching is fresh manna and we need it to grow spiritually. Principles that were not taught to you previously can have a very positive impact on situations and change the course of your life.

However, if there is a bully preacher you watch on TV or where you attend, go to God first and ask the Holy Spirit to reveal the truth to you and to the preacher as well.

I have gained much insight from pastors and teachers over my life that has altered the entire course of me and my family's destiny. You may not be the person you want to be, but without an anointed pastor or minister in your life, the struggle to become all that you can be in God will be even greater. Be cautious of the self-absorbed and self-promoting preachers who bully you and make you feel guilty if you don't do what they ask. Be on alert for manipulating tactics used in ministries to pay the mortgages of multi-million dollar homes, Leer jets, and fancy cars when there is a much better use of funds to advance His Kingdom and help the hurting.

I was fortunate in life to live with a father who was a minister and didn't have a bullying bone in his body. He was a great role model and example of Christ to the world. He was compassionate and lived what he preached and never compromised.

I have a good friend, however, whose father was a minister and also a bully—not necessarily to his parishioners, but to his family. He was physically and verbally abusive until eventually his behavior destroyed his ministry and marriage. My friend grew up with some major dysfunctions, but was an overcomer and today is successful and a loving, kind man. He's a perfect example of how God can take something toxic and turn it into something good. He is now influencing the lives of thousands of people through his ministry and acts of kindness.

Friend, if you have been bullied in the past by someone in leadership or authority, forget the past, forgive them, and let God turn it around to your favor. His plan is to see you succeed in life and live in peace and joy, so don't hold onto a grudge or bitterness in your heart. Release the hurt, shame, and anger and watch the blessings of almighty God begin to fulfill your life.

Establish a Relationship

Scripture warns us against being foolish and gullible, and most often those who use these television ministers as their church fall prey to these fraudulent ministries. When we don't have accountability with a local church where we give and can ask for financial reports, we end up supporting crooks. And we should never respond in guilt and give more than we are able.

The Bible says we should give within our means with a cheerful heart.

> 2 Corinthians 8:11,12 *"And here is my judgment about what is best for you in this matter. Last year you were the first not only to give but also to have the desire to do so. Now finish the work, so that your eager willingness to do it may be matched by your completion of it, **according to your means.**" (NIV)*

> 2 Corinthians 9:7 *"Each of you should **give what you have decided in your heart to give, not reluctantly or under compulsion**, for God loves a cheerful giver." (NIV)*

I've had people tell me that if they gave 10% of their income (or the tithe), they wouldn't have food to feed their family or pay other bills such as utilities, car payments etc. In some situations, that may well be true. Well, then you must do what the above scripture states. Ask the Lord what He would have you do. Perhaps there are places in your budget where you can cut back. Sometimes our wants overtake our needs. If your employer said you must either take a 10% drop in pay or lose your job, which would you choose? And if you decided to keep the job, what would you have to change about your lifestyle to afford to live on your new income? Trust me, His Kingdom will be advanced with or without your tithe.

How Much is Too Much?

Part of the reason why we struggle with tithes and offerings is a faith issue. We don't believe God can meet all our needs according to His riches in Glory with 90% of our income. Once we begin being faithful in what we can give, watch what God will do in our lives. He can promote us, increase us financially, and bring us to a place where we can give 10%, 20% or more. I know of individuals who actually give over 20% of their income to the work of God and they are very blessed financially. It's a heart and faith issue when we give. We must examine the motive behind why we give—or why we don't—and allow God to make our hearts pure when making donations.

On the other side of the coin, and in direct opposition to the scripture, I've watched a family give 10% of their income to the local church because of fear or judgment, and then let their bills fall behind to the point where they eventually file for bankruptcy. They ended up losing their home and will have bad credit for a long time. This is not glorifying to God. He tells us not to steal from Him—how can He possibly be pleased if we steal from the mortgage company or the utility company by taking money meant to pay those bills and giving them to the church in His name?

Part of the problem is that people frivolously spend beyond their means, allowing their wants to outpace their needs. Or perhaps they have been manipulated or shamed into giving, and simply have nowhere else to get the money.

If this is your situation, stop. Ask God for forgiveness in our lack of unwise stewardship. We must renounce bad spending habits and change our spending habits. God is faithful to forgive us and can get us easily back on the right track. Struggle is not God's plan for us. We must ask Him for direction. We must be in agreement with our spouse in the matter. Giving is a heart issue, not a money matter. So many times Christians get hung up about being afraid of being under a curse as Malachi speaks of in the Old Testament. Hey, I've got some good news for you; you are no longer under a curse because Christ made us free from the curse of the law. But that doesn't mean there is no law. Jesus said He didn't come to abolish the law, but to fulfill it. This means that even when we don't measure up in terms of tithes and offerings, He has already paid the price. No excuses, no get-out-of-jail-free cards, but no condemnation, either.

"Christ redeemed us from the curse of the law by becoming a curse for us, for it is written: 'Cursed is everyone who is hung on a pole'." Galatians 3:13 (NIV)

When our hearts are right and we plant a seed with faith and a grateful heart, God will do his part and bring increase. I heard of a man who desired to make a certain amount of money. He started tithing based upon the amount of money he wanted to make someday. Before long, he was making that exact amount! I personally have tested this out and it has worked. I was at a place early in my career and wanted to make a certain amount of money so I started tithing on that desired salary amount. It was very shortly after I received a promotion and a raise that took me to that level of income. If you're struggling financially consider selling something to pay off debt or maybe get a second part time job. You could even have a garage sale or place some unused items on EBay or Craig's List to get caught up.

Being in the banking and finance business for many years, I have reviewed numerous tax returns on corporations and individuals. I have noticed that individuals who give to non-profits every year always seem to make it through the recessions and tough economic cycles that the rest of us as well go through periodically. Even businessmen that don't profess faith in God that give financially seem to always be ahead of some of the others. This spiritual and physical law of planting and sowing works for all, believers and non-believers. The main difference is that the believer is helping to advance Christ Kingdom and lives in inner peace and joy to a great extent!

Chapter Fourteen

Bully Teachers

*"And he gave some, apostles; and some, prophets; and some, evangelists; and some, pastors and **teachers**; for the **perfecting of the saints.**" Ephesians 4:11-12 (KJV)*

When I was young and foolish and had a smart mouth, I had a teacher tell me to shut up or he was going to slap my face. This was back in the early 80's when teachers could still get away with saying or possibly even doing this. His statement struck such fear in me I haven't forgot his words even to this day. Today however, a teacher who threatened a student in this way would probably lose their jobs and never teach again with all the political correctness in the world. Although the threat he made to me was wrong, it still made me have a fear of him because he was a bully and what was I going to do?

Wherever there are teachers, there is some kind of politics, whether that be in schools, colleges, churches, or wherever there are teachers. They have favorites and they use their authority to humiliate, criticize, and destroy their students.

Teachers can have a life-long effect on their students. Their victims are often fearful of retaliation if it is addressed with someone above them. Today we are also seeing a reverse of this where teachers are being bullied with students threatening them physically. This stems from a society that lacks the core family values and teachings of showing respect for those in authority.

Teachers often punish their students or use manipulating tactics to force them into doing something they don't want to do. Colleges are especially known for this because liberal teachers force their agenda on conservative students, even giving lower grades if they do not buy into their beliefs and agenda. They intimidate students with contrary beliefs and by encouraging immorality or denying there are consequences for sin. We see this more and more not only in colleges, but even in high school, junior high, and elementary schools. This is a major reason for the moral decline in our society.

Stand firm in your values and don't compromise because of pressure or being perceived as a bigot or uninformed. We will likely all face situations where we'll be asked to give in to a contrary doctrine of morality. We must stand up to this type of bully. When you maintain your principles and values, you are not promised from God that everyone is going to run and love you. Quite the opposite can be true. Be of good cheer though because you can overcome the world and the secular teaching that goes against the truth and words of almighty God.

A large majority of universities in this country are pushing a very liberal agenda that does not line up with the word of God. We are being forced to accept immorality and unbiblical ways of life at an alarming rate. If we resist and argue these worldviews, we are labeled as homophobic, racist, close-minded, or bigots, yet these people demonstrate their close-mindedness when they don't accept our biblical truths. Doesn't that make them bigots themselves?

Unfortunately, tolerance in society and major universities doesn't go both ways. We must stand for the truth of God's word even when it's not popular.

If you hold to conservative views and values, you will be perceived as unlearned and intolerant. Professors love to embarrass students who do not agree with their political views. Because of their title and position they exhibit a self-absorbed "know it all" attitude wherein they can do or say no wrong, and their views are absolute truth. This is ironic because many do not even believe in absolute values or morality. Many of these teachers have no belief system at all or don't even believe in "absolute" right and wrong.

Not all teachers are bullies. God places teachers in our life to increase us in wisdom and understanding on a topic or subject that can make a major difference in our life. Unfortunately, there are abusive and manipulative teachers that convince many Christians to buy into their liberal God-hating, humanistic agenda.

When we consider the impact this has on our society and our world, we can't help but see how detrimental it has been to the moral decay of our culture. Stay the course and don't waiver in your principles. Don't allow bully teachers to manipulate you or embarrass you in front of others. Be strong and fight the good fight of faith. Look for others to support you and stand for truth alongside you. There is power in numbers, and sometimes engaging other believers in this type of environment can advance the cause and change others for the good. Be strong and knowledgeable to defend your case and positions. If you are well prepared to answer when tough questions are asked, you will gain credibility and may even sway others, including the teacher.

When it's all said and done, always show respect and give soft answers. Stay on point, and don't allow the discussion to veer off on a tangent. If you are dealing with a bully teacher, you don't want to be a bully yourself. Nobody deserves to be bullied in a classroom by a teacher who holds different beliefs or is just an all-out abuser.

There may come a time when you need to involve authorities at a higher level. If you still aren't able to resolve the issue, you may need to move to a different school. If you choose to stand firm, show respect and never compromise. You will leave a mark and influence others even though you don't see it at the time.

Choose to think the best of people even when they don't agree with you. There are many who will not agree with the Bible or believe in God. They will ask "if there's a God then why do children die of disease or why did so many lose their life in that tsunami or hurricane? Why is there evil?" Teachers who are self-promoting bullies love to throw these questions at believers.

We don't know the mind of God and the truth is there is an evil force at work in the world today that inflicts pain and suffering that cannot be justified by anyone. Most will agree that love is a true ethic, and if there is love, there must be freedom of choice. If you truly love someone, you will not force your will upon them, but will allow them to choose. This is one of the greatest gifts God has given. With that, unfortunately, comes the ability to choose good or evil. There will always be those who choose evil. There are logical consequences of choice. It can be difficult when you are going through pain, sorrow, or suffering to understand this and we will not always understand events that occur in life. God tells us in His word that His thought and ways are higher than ours. We will not always understand why certain things happen in life. Don't spend your life angry and bitter at God when the devil may actually be the one to blame or even yourself for the un-wise choices we make. That's where we must learn to pray every day and ask for protection and His angels to watch over us!

Surround yourself with believers who will trust God with you to bring you through those trials. There is evil because there is choice. This is not to say someone chooses sickness or disease, but possibly through generational curses, words spoken unintentionally, or toxic thoughts, we allow bitterness, anger, or a grudge that can produce sickness.

There are scriptural references to causes of sickness, one of which is sin, otherwise Jesus would have never said, "go and sin no more" after He healed a person. Often the curse is planted unknowingly. In the case of a very young child, a parent must stand in the gap, cover their children with the blood of Jesus, and speak life over them and protection.

There are some questions in life, however, we will not have the answer to until we get to the other side. Seek God with all your heart and continue to believe. Sometimes we go through things in life because we bring them on ourselves, and God is trying to get our attention so we can spend time with Him. Maybe we haven't been seeking Him or talking to Him as much and He misses our company.

Other times there are no answers to circumstances. We can spend the rest of our life being angry at God because we don't understand why such and such happened or we can trust that God has a plan and His ways are higher than ours. God is eternal, all knowing, and does not live in time as we do. Our finite minds are not going to understand some issues and circumstances which are eternal in nature. Someone once said when we get to Heaven we will understand why certain things happened. That may be true, but when we all get to Heaven, we may not even care at that point.

The person of Jesus Christ HAS changed lives and He continues to do so. When drugs which mask problems no longer work because our bodies become immune to them, only Christ can give you total freedom from that addiction or problem you face. When Adam and Eve sinned, the scripture tells us that man turned the power to rule the earth back over to the devil. People blame God for evil when they should be blaming the devil.

The great news is through the atoning blood and sacrifice of Jesus, we can appropriate that power to live a kingdom life that brings life, health, and prosperity. Don't allow non-believing teachers to bully you, but know how to defend your faith and walk in boldness. Don't worry if you don't see them come to Christ. Some will reject Him and that is very sad because God does not wish that any would perish as the Bible tells us. Our choices are powerful, so trust that God has a purpose and destiny that will impact eternity.

Chapter Fifteen
Turn the Other Cheek—Most of the Time

"Even fools are thought wise if they keep silent, and discerning if they hold their tongues." Proverbs 17:28 (NIV)

The book of Proverbs is not telling us we should never speak up. There are times when we must defend our position and hold our ground, especially in terms of values, moral, and ethical situations. What this scripture says is that most of the time, we need to stay quiet and not start babbling and end up with our foot in our mouth.

I have been in that situation and have said things I shouldn't have said. Sometimes things we say hurt others and wound them deeply beyond immediate repair. Thankfully, it's not the end of the world and there is grace sufficient for even our biggest mistakes. God always gives a second chance and a third chance and even more. His grace covers over all of our shortcomings, so don't be discouraged when you feel you have messed up. Learn from your mistake, get up, and move forward with your life. God has great things in store for you.

There are times, however, when we must take a stance, sometimes even physically fighting back. Self-defense techniques, such as many of the mixed martial arts programs, can at least give us a feeling of security that we can defend ourselves or our loved ones if needed.

We live in a dangerous world, and we can't be so naïve to think that everywhere we go we are safe.

There is evil in this world. One way to stay out of these situations is to pray and ask God to keep you safe. However, when you're a kid in school and someone punches you in the face, you are going to have a tough time talking your way out of a fight. Panic and fear can immobilize a person in confrontational situations. Take a deep breath and remain focused. Do everything you can to walk away, but if there is no other choice, you must decide to run or fight. Running is not cowardice, and may be the best decision at the time. If you can avoid a physical confrontation, choose that path. There is no value in ending up injured, or injuring somebody else.

Often you can defuse an angry person by remaining calm and apologizing for the misunderstanding. Keep your distance but watch their body actions closely to avoid contact. Talk to God through the process. This is where prayer without ceasing comes to mind and can help. Other times you must defend yourself and ask God for strength. I have seen where praying in the spirit defused dangerous situations. Sometimes praying in the spirit with groanings that come from deep within that you don't understand, but God knows exactly what you're saying deep inside. Romans 8:26 (NIV) *"In the same way, the Spirit helps us in our weakness. We do not know what we ought to pray for, but the Spirit himself intercedes for us through wordless groans."* I am convinced from my own experience that this works. The devil does not know what you are saying and cannot intercept these prayers that go directly to the throne of Almighty God on your behalf!

Learning to negotiate is essential in these situations, but not always practical. Angry individuals are not mentally or rationally stable nor are they thinking clearly, especially if there are drugs and/or alcohol involved. However, praying in the spirit can break the evil forces and spiritual powers being demonstrated. People who don't believe that praying in the spirit is for today are missing a very key element in walking in faith and kingdom living. I know the supernatural works through the situation and until you experience it yourself you may not understand this gift. The scripture tells us in I Corinthians 2:14 (KJV) *"But the natural man receiveth not the things of the Spirit of God: for they are foolishness unto him: neither can he know them, because they are spiritually discerned."* You have nothing to lose by trying this approach the next time you are the victim in a bullying situation. The word of God says that you will be given power after the Holy Spirit comes upon you. Many people live beneath their privileges because of fear of the Holy Spirit or what we called growing up in Pentecost as the Holy Ghost! A ghost is something that appears from someone that died. Well friend Jesus died for you but lives again and His spirit now wants to come live in you and assist you with the bullies of life! Allow Him to come and possess you with supernatural power! I live a supernatural life and would have never gotten here without the Holy Ghost living and residing inside of me and speaking through me. It's a great feeling walking through a dark alley without a single stitch of fear! All because I know who lives in me and protects me.

> *"The LORD is with me; I will not be afraid. What can mere mortals do to me? "Psalms 118:6 (NIV)*

Staying in a group and limiting yourself to safe settings are important. Avoid environments that generate strife and danger. Although I say I am not afraid to walk in a dark alley, it's not something I go around doing all the time or recommend. That's stupidity. Sometimes however we go through dark alleys of life and find ourself in a situation we weren't looking to get into. Don't get yourself in a tough situation because of a bad decision on your part. If you pray every day and ask God Almighty for protection in your life, He will honor your prayers. When we are walking in His ways and obeying God's word for our life, no enemy stands a chance.

Praying the blood of Jesus and summoning His angels to watch over you and your family supernaturally brings powerful protection against any forces. You can learn to remain calm in the midst of storms and violent environments when you pray God's supernatural protection over your life.

Being calm, cool, and collected is a great way to live your life

When I was younger, it seemed I was always getting myself in situations that were not good. Sometimes I had a chip on my shoulder, or maybe someone looked at me the wrong way, or I stared them down. No matter what the reason or the behavior, I ended up in fighting situations.

Never smart.

Sometimes it takes a while for us to grow up, but one of the benefits is we gain insight and wisdom into living a life of calm and peace versus strife and fighting. It's much better on our health and relationships with others. You must *"cast all your anxiety on him"*, the scriptures declare, *"for He cares for you"* I Peter 5:7 (NIV). We can turn life's tough situations over to God and let Him work them out for us. The scripture also says that we should submit to God and resist the devil and he will flee from us. The key is submitting to God. When we pray in our quiet time—mine is in the morning—we should say, "God, I submit every aspect of my life to You: my mind, will, emotions, and direction for my life".

The incredible feeling of being calm, cool, and collected is a great way to live your life. Being anxious and nervous is no way to live and is physically bad for your health.

If you can avoid yelling and screaming and learn to take a deep breath in stressful times, life will go so much better for you. Shrug your shoulders a few times and relax. Squeeze your fists and then let them relax. There are many techniques that can help bring down your blood pressure and stress level.

We hear the saying, "don't let your emotions control you". Well that's fine if you're a robot, but God built us with emotions and you can't always control them like you'd like to. You will discover that when you do make an effort to control them the best you can, it will put less demand on your body and mind. One of the reasons I work out is to stay in shape and stay healthy, but the other reason is that it helps relieve stress and detoxify your body. When you exercise and sweat, chemicals are released from your body that can be damaging to you physically. When I lay off working out, especially around the holidays as we get so busy, I don't feel as well and am a bit sluggish. As I get back into it, however, my energy levels increase and I feel and stay healthy.

The fruit of the spirit begins with Love, Joy, and Peace. When we exhibit these characteristics, it is harder for us to get into situations where we even have to think about turning the other cheek. Walking in love as Christ did sounds impossible, but with His spirit living inside of us, we can do anything. When we learn to put on the whole armor of God, we can withstand any attacks. Paul tells us that we "do not wrestle against flesh and blood, but against principalities, powers, rulers of darkness and spiritual wickedness in high places".

As we do this and stand in faith and prayer, God will protect us. He will be a fence around you that no one can cross and harm you. Speak His word in your prayers and the devil will flee. When you go through the fiery trials of life, you can rest assured that you will not be burnt, you won't even come out smelling of smoke, but you will come out as pure gold!

Top left: Born December 25, 1965, they brought me to my mother in a red stocking. Dad moved us from Phoenix, AZ to Appleton, WI where he pastored his first church The Tabernacle of Praise, Medina, WI – Top middle third one in. Bottom left I'm the one at the bottom and bottom right I'm the one at the far left. That church had raspberry bushes behind it that we enjoyed as kids.

Meeting the love of my life at Evangel University top left. I fell in love the first time we met. Competing and placing in an all-natural body building competition. Having three boys, there's never been a dull moment. They have brought great joy to our life. We have lived with super heroes for many years and always felt safe.

Top left - family picture at Carter Lake. Top right CSU MBA graduation with mom, mother and father in law and aunt Mary.
Bottom left - Bronco game with my posse and bottom right - Christmas time in the Rockies

Chapter Sixteen
Mom's Miracle

"The tongue has the power of life and death, and those who love it will eat its fruit." Proverbs 18:21 (NIV)

I will never forget the sound of my sister's voice trembling when she called with the news that Mom had been diagnosed with cancer. Yet on the inside, I felt something rise up within me that I'll describe as holy anger. I was angry! Not at my mother or anyone else, but angry at the devil because he thought his wimpy little self could try this on my mom.

On the other hand, there was a sense of compassion for my mom that she was in a fight and I was in Colorado while she was in a hospital bed in Texas. I so badly wanted to be there with her. Growing up in a close family meant we learned to stick together and fight together. My older sister Sandra used to fight for me and stand up for me when I was bullied and full of fear as a young man. Now she and my sister Rhonda were there with my mother fighting on her behalf, and their brothers Kevin and David were about to arrive as re-enforcers to help in the battle. When we join forces in agreement, the bully devil's plan begins to be shaken and crumble to the ground!

I have always known that we can live beyond the impossible and experience the supernatural power of God in our life. Living by faith means we must take risk. Completely trusting in the work of the cross and the precious blood of Jesus is a must when dealing with adversity. Matthew tells us that "ALL things are possible with God."

Sometimes, however, we must change something in our life. Sometimes we expose ourselves or open the door to something that can bring sickness, disease, financial lack, or destruction. Most of the time we do this without even knowing it and then we wonder why we can't get victory. We have to deal with the root of the problem and often we don't know what that is. We can, however, ask the Holy Spirit to reveal things to us and then begin our fight.

> I Corinthians 2:10 says, *"these are the things God has revealed to us by his Spirit. The Spirit searches all things, even the deep things of God."(NIV)*

> John 16:13 says, *"But when he, the Spirit of truth, comes, he will guide you into all the truth. He will not speak on his own; he will speak only what he hears, and he will tell you what is yet to come."(NIV)*

I couldn't understand, as many of us don't, how the devil could be allowed to put a disease such as cancer upon my mother. She was one of the most God-fearing women I have ever known. She didn't live in sin, she was kind, she loved others, and was especially in tuned with God in her prayer life. She had seen angels in her home during a time of worship she was having. Unknowingly though, there was a root to this attack–a door was opened. They told her it was a cancerous tumor that was around her ovaries, uterus, and had spread all throughout her pelvic region. Apparently, the surgeon who did the exploratory surgery had diagnosed it as colon cancer from its growth pattern. He said it was too large and had spread too much to even try to remove.

Before Steffani took me to the airport to fly to Texas, I asked her to pray with me and help me to ask the Holy Spirit what was the cause of this and what door was opened to manifest this attack. As we prayed and asked the Holy Spirit to reveal to us why, I didn't feel a thing. I didn't get any divine revelation. No words came to my mind and I didn't hear any small soft voice. That's why God put Steffani in my life as she is especially sensitive to hearing the Holy Spirit speak!

I asked Steffani if she heard anything or if she was getting anything and she said, "The only thing I keep hearing is abandonment." Abandonment? I thought back to what I knew of her childhood. I said, "I don't understand. My mom was never abandoned". Then Steff said, "well, remember what your momma said when your daddy died? Your mom said "what am I ever going to do without your dad? "

When my dad died, it was extremely painful to our family. He was an incredible pillar of spiritual strength in all our lives and especially our mom. He never let her take out the trash or put gas in the car, and still at 73, opened the car door for her. He treated her like a queen. She may not have recognized it at the time, but there were feelings of being abandoned, and the root cause of that is fear.

As I boarded the plane, I asked the Holy Spirit to show me how to pray when I got there. I felt like the Lord told me to ask my mom how she wanted us to pray. To receive a miracle, there must be agreement and unity amongst the parties involved. There were several occasions when mom had said "well, maybe it's my time to go be with the Lord and see your dad again." Some folks get tired of fighting this life and often get a glimpse into what is on the other side. When that happens, many times their mind is made up and they are ready to graduate to heaven. That's not a bad option!

When I arrived in the hospital room, my sisters, brother, niece and her fiancé were all there. I hugged and greeted my mother and we had some small talk about what the doctor's report was. Then I asked my mom, "mom, how do you want us to pray? Because of statements you made prior about going to see the Lord and going to see dad, I want to make sure we are in complete unity."

We can pray until we're blue in the face and pass out, but if there is no unity, nothing will happen. I knew a man whose wife had been diagnosed with cancer and he kept telling her, "I release you to go to heaven", when the whole time she was believing God for a miracle. She died believing for a miracle because her husband's faith lay in another direction. There must be unity when you are standing in faith for healing and miracles.

I said, "Mom, do you believe God has more for you to do here on earth or do you want to go home?" She said, "I believe He has more for me to do here." I said, "okay, then, turn off the TV, let's play some scripture music that a friend of mine had produced and everyone here needs to believe God will heal and completely restore mom to health."

As I prayed, I told the evil demonic spirit of cancer to leave her body. I commanded the door of fear and feelings of abandonment to be dismissed forever. We closed every plan of the devil against her health and began to pray in the spirit and declare that by the blood and stripes of Jesus on the cross she was healed. We prayed fervently as the scripture says in James 5:16 *"The effectual fervent prayer of a righteous man availeth much." (KJV)*

After we prayed, Mom said it felt like warm oil was running down her entire body. We'd felt the power of God while we were praying, but we kept fighting using scripture. The word of God must be incorporated into our prayer life to make effective prayers. Jesus used the word of God against the devil after he had fasted for forty days in the wilderness, and the devil left him alone. I looked up every scripture on healing I could and read them aloud to my mother. Some of them were the following:

James 5:15 *"And the prayer offered in faith will make the sick person well; the Lord will raise them up."(NIV)*

Proverbs 4:20-22 *"My son, pay attention to what I say; listen closely to my words.*

21. Do not let them out of your sight, keep them within your heart; 22. for they are life to those who find them and health to a man's whole body." (NIV)

Isaiah 53:5 *"But he was pierced for our transgressions, he was crushed for our iniquities; the punishment that brought us peace was upon him, and by his wounds we are healed." (NIV)*

Psalms 103:2, 3 *"Praise the LORD, O my soul, and forget not all his benefits--*

3. who forgives all your sins and heals all your diseases." (NIV)

Mark 11:23 *"Truly I tell you, if anyone says to this mountain, 'Go, throw yourself into the sea,' and does not doubt in their heart but believes that what they say will happen, it will be done for them." (NIV)*

John 14:12 *"Very truly I tell you, whoever believes in me will do the works I have been doing, and they will do even greater things than these, because I am going to the Father." (NIV)*

Luke 1:37 *"For nothing is impossible with God." (NLT)*

Matthew 19:26 *"But Jesus looked at them and said, "With man this is impossible, but with God all things are possible." (ESV)*

Mark 10:27 *"Jesus looked at them and said, "With man it is impossible, but not with God. For all things are possible with God." (ESV)*

Mark 11:24 *"Therefore I say unto you, what things soever ye desire, when ye pray, believe that ye receive them, and ye shall have them." (KJV)*

I John 3:22 *"and receive from him anything we ask, because we keep his commands and do what pleases him." (NIV)*

I John 5:14 *"This is the confidence we have in approaching God: that if we ask anything according to his will, he hears us." (NIV)*

You get the point. There are numerous scriptures on healing, asking, receiving, and miracles that are promised to us. I read scriptures aloud through the night as my mother fell asleep. My sister read scriptures the next day. I told my mom, "if anything specific jumps out at you as we read, hold on to it and focus on it in your mind".

The word tells us we must renew the spirit of our mind. When I pray for people, I ask God to renew the spirit of their mind to activate their faith, which enables them to receive their healing. When people aren't healed, there are several reasons why: (1) they don't always believe; (2) they may have something in their heart in terms of bitterness, unforgiveness, or anger that is withholding their miracle; (3) sometimes folks have exposed themselves to new age or demonic, spiritual books, movies, or recordings that can open a door and loose evil upon them; and (4) people are tired and ready to go to heaven.

If you're not getting your healing or miracle it is NOT God's fault. He already paid a tremendous price through His Son Jesus on the cross. It is our place to stand in agreement with the word of God and not waiver. I have told people I prayed for who didn't get healed right away to not give up the day before their miracle. Many times we get tired and our faith dwindles and is weakened. Friend, the devil is the biggest bully we will ever face, and he comes to kill, steal, and destroy. Jesus came to bring life and bring it more abundantly. Abundant life is not having cancer or living in poverty.

A couple days after this prayer and scripture marathon, I needed to return to Colorado as my family and I had prior vacation plans the next week to fly to Cabo San Lucas. I just recently obtained my MBA and the vacation was my reward for all the hard work. It was a great vacation by the way as I caught an 8 foot 7 inch blue marlin while deep sea fishing! I was torn, however, between staying with Mom and leaving, but she assured me she had a good handle on the prayer and scripture reading, and with all the other family around her, she was going to fight.

Before I flew out though the doctors were going to do a colonoscopy to locate the origin of the cancer so they could initiate a treatment plan. Even though my mother had told me she didn't want to go through radiation or chemotherapy, the doctors still needed to present a game plan. After a while, a doctor came out and said, "David, here are the pictures of your mom's colon, and I'm not sure what the surgeon saw, but I don't see any cancer."

I knew we didn't need a test. We already knew she was healed. But we were glad to learn that God had astounded the doctors again. However, this doctor didn't want to say my mother was clear of cancer until she conferred with Mom's oncologist, which she couldn't do until the next day.

While we were at a layover at the Dallas airport the next day on our way to Cabo, my son was surfing Facebook. He said, "Dad look. Aunt Rhonda just posted that all the doctors had declared Nanna cancer free!" I immediately called my sister and she stated that the doctors had come in after further tests and said they could not explain it, but there was no more tumor in her body. Her blood test showed no signs of cancer! Praise God! She said the doctor threw up his hands in disbelief and said, "I can't explain it. I held that tumor in my hands but couldn't remove it and it's gone now!"

Well, we knew what happened. Although the doctors didn't understand, we knew that we serve a God of miracles, and He can do the same for you, my friend, if you are facing a battle in your life. Whether it is cancer, diabetes, kidney failure, or a crippling disorder, you can be free from this. You may have anxiety, depression, or other mental disorders, but God is ready and able to set you free right now. Your finances may be strained, you may be considering filing bankruptcy, but God can restore your finances and release abundant blessing in your money situation. Your marriage may be a disaster or you may be considering divorce, but God is standing by waiting to restore your relationship better than it ever was.

Ask and you will receive.

Believe in your heart that He can change the course of your life, health, marriage, and money.

Your destiny is to live a long healthy life, blessed financially and in your relationships. Abundant life is yours for the taking. Don't let the bully devil steal your joy any longer. You may be going through a test, but you will have a testimony when it's over. Don't give up a day before your miracle. God is getting ready to change the course of your life.

Sometimes we go through tough times, but keep in mind you will be stronger and better off when you've come through the fiery trials. You will come though like pure gold through the refiner's fire. Hang on and don't lose sight of what great things are ahead for you.

You reap what you sow, so my suggestion to you that has worked for me and many others is this:

- Stay plugged into a good Bible-believing church and give to God–let it come from your heart's desire to advance His Kingdom.
- Read your Bible every day–this is often how God will speak to you. Psalms, Proverbs, and the epistles of Paul are good, too, for your daily walk.
- Pray. If you're married, pray every day with your spouse. Husbands be the leader and initiate this.
- Practice daily affirmations such as: I am healthy, I am wealthy, I am favored, I walk in wisdom, I am successful, I have supernatural knowledge, I am self-controlled, I am disciplined, I am financially free, I am a miracle worker, etc.
- Renew the spirit of your mind during a quiet time, preferably in the morning, by removing toxic thoughts aloud and replacing them with scriptures that counteract the negative thoughts.
- Use your talents and grow them to bless the Lord and the body of Christ. If God has put a desire in you to do something you dream of, pursue it with all you have in you.
- Exercise and eat right. It's okay to splurge once in a while, but practice self-control.
- Have a good work ethic and don't be lazy.
- Think and speak only positive thoughts and words.

Obviously, this isn't an all-inclusive recipe, but it's pretty easy and doesn't take too much effort. It's not rocket science, so give it a try! It can have a drastic impact on your life if there's even just one of the activities above that you aren't doing and begin to incorporate them in your life.

Chapter Seventeen

Dad's Heritage

"May God give you heaven's dew and earth's richness —an abundance of grain and new wine. May nations serve you and peoples bow down to you. Be lord over your brothers, and may the sons of your mother bow down to you. May those who curse you be cursed and those who bless you be blessed." Genesis 27:28-29 (NIV)

Almost a year before my father passed away, I had a strong desire to ask for his blessing. I knew and experienced his prayers over us as children and even over my own family after Steff and I married. In the Bible, when a father spoke a blessing, it was very significant and prophetic over his children.

I wanted his blessing over me memorialized, and today these words, written in his own handwriting, hang in my office. Even though the words are faded and are hard to read, this piece of paper is worth more to me than any stock certificate worth millions hanging alongside it.

The above scripture is Isaac's blessing over Jacob. And although the blessing truly belonged to Esau and was stolen from him, the blessing itself was still granted to Jacob. To me, it is the story of Father God and how salvation isn't fair. We don't deserve grace and mercy at all, like the prodigal son who went and spent his entire inheritance and then came home. His father ran to meet him. It's the only scripture that shows God running. Why? For his son who had left and spent everything he had on worldly pleasures and then ended up broke and living in a pig's pen.

The father's older son didn't understand all the excitement and was upset at how his father welcomed his son who had turned his back on the family and left to pursue evil desires, but the Father explained that his lost son had come home and that he, the older son, still had all the blessings given him and that would never change.

A man once told me he was unsavable! Friend, that is just not true. He was a wealthy banker and was living to please himself, but also felt he had too much sin to overcome. The scriptures say, *"If you declare with your mouth, 'Jesus is Lord,' and believe in your heart that God raised him from the dead, you will be saved." Romans 10:9 (NIV).* That makes salvation pretty easy. It requires us only to believe and nothing else.

When Jesus was dying on the cross He said *"it is finished"* meaning there is nothing you can add to grant you salvation. You will never be good enough and will always have a sinful nature. Ecclesiastes 7:20 (NIV) says *"There is not a righteous man on earth who does what is right and never sins".* The truth is we all have a sin nature and our salvation has nothing to do with what we do in terms of works. It's about what He did on the cross and accepting that for our redemption.

> *"Indeed, there is no one on earth who is righteous, no one who does what is right and never sins." Ecclesiastes 7:20 (NIV)*

The denomination I was raised in taught we had to do what Acts 2:38 (KJV) said to get to Heaven. We had to repent, be baptized in Jesus' name, receive the Holy Ghost, and speak in tongues, or we were not going to heaven. It never said anything about going to hell after that verse, but that is what I was taught to believe. Manmade doctrine from one scripture can be dangerous and bondage in your life.

In addition to that, girls and women were not allowed to cut their hair, we couldn't go to dances or movies, and if you drank or smoked, you were hell bound for sure.

What about John 3:16? (NIV) *"For God so loved the world that he gave his one and only Son, that whoever believes in him shall not perish but have eternal life".*

We have made salvation and getting to heaven a hard thing when Jesus already did the hard thing for us. Believing is easy and declaring with our mouth is not hard.

When we understand the father's love for us, it makes life so much more pleasant and bearable. I always felt condemned. Always felt I was headed to hell. What a terrible way to live. Thankfully my dad was a loving father who didn't condemn me. He loved his family and others as I have never seen another man love. They say that many children get their impressions of Father God from the way their earthly father treated them. I was fortunate enough to have a great role model in my father. He was a praying man and came from praying parents. My grandparents prayed every day for their kids and all their grandkids. They called them all by name and spoke blessing over them.

If you're saying, "well, David, I didn't have that so where does that leave me?", know this: there is a heavenly Father who can replace the emptiness and void you may have had in your earthly father. Whether he was there, but just not engaged, maybe abusive, or not there at all, Father God can fill the void. Just ask him to!

The Bible talks about generational curses that can bring negative consequences to our life because of the sins and iniquities of our forefathers back three and four generations before us. Many people do not realize the significance of this and the impact to our lives, health, money, marriage, lifespan, and children. A root of bitterness from a great-great-grandfather could cause cancer or lust in our life, and we might not realize it.

Now, I know this sounds crazy, but is there something you are dealing with right now that you can't seem to get victory over? I heard a pastor talk about how he struggled with lust even while he was preaching and seeing a beautiful woman in the audience. He asked the Lord why and God told him there was a root of bitterness from someone in his past generational bloodline. Once he dealt with it and commanded it to release off of him in the Name and by the blood of Jesus, he was completely free.

Sometimes, we have allowed ourselves to be exposed to evil desires through varies sources; books, tv, movies, new age speakers. We must guard our heart as it is the wellspring of life as Proverbs tells us. Our heavenly Father hears when we pray, but the word also says that *"If I had cherished sin in my heart, the Lord would not have listened"* Psalms 66:18 (NIV) and it also says *"Surely the arm of the LORD is not too short to save, nor his ear too dull to hear. But your iniquities have separated you from your God; your sins have hidden his face from you, so that he will not hear."* Isaiah 59:1-2. (NIV)

There are reasons our prayers don't get answered or we don't feel like we hear from the Father God. Out of naivety, we do things unaware or we open doors that create evil desires causing us to sin which stops our promised blessings.

Many of the issues we deal with are rooted in fear, anger, bitterness, strife, and jealousy. Once we close the door to these and loose it from our life in the Name and by the blood of Jesus, we can be set free and delivered. Then we can see God move in our life in a new dimension.

Friend, we are saved by grace as Ephesians tells us, but to live kingdom living here on earth we need to take steps to release anger and fear and other toxic feelings in our lives. Our heavenly Father is waiting for us to come to him with a pure heart and clean hands.

This is not to say He never listens to the sinner, but if you are not getting the breakthrough you seek in your life, go to God with a repentant heart and see what happens. Many times we need to ask the Holy Spirit to reveal to us issues that we are completely unaware of or we have hidden deep in the crevasses of our heart from many years back.

My dad believed in praying in Jesus' Name and applying the blood of Jesus to every area of his life. When the children of Israel were getting ready to leave Egypt, they applied the lamb's blood to the doorpost so that the death angel would not come in and kill their firstborn. Today we have the precious blood of Jesus Christ that we can use to appropriate protection over our family.

Steffani and I pray every morning and I state in our prayer that we cover Zach, Tayler, Tyler Derek, Steff, and me with the blood of Jesus. Something happens in the spiritual realm when you pray this way. Many people don't do this and they miss out on a great blessing in their life.

I can hear my dad even now pleading the blood of Jesus over his kids' lives. My father-in-law does the same over all our families. What a rich heritage Steffani and I have been blessed with.

There is nothing more powerful in the entire universe than the blood of Jesus. When you pray in His Name and apply his blood over your life, get ready for miracles, blessing, protection, and favor to overwhelm you!

Our heavenly Father wants to bless us. It is His desire to see you prosper and live in divine health. It's time we start taking back our money, our marriage, our health, and our children that the devil has stolen. There is such significance to words we speak over our lives. That's why when I was compelled to ask my earthly father for his blessing. I knew it would mean something and would cause a reaction in the spirit that many don't understand. Our mouths and the words we speak are creative forces. My father wrote these words to me about a year before he passed away and I will forever treasure them:

David,

Through your offspring, multitudes will be blessed. Always walk in God's love and His presence. The Lord God will give you wisdom and knowledge as you walk in the counsel of the Godly. The Lord God Almighty shall command the blessing upon you, and all that you set your hand to do. He shall make you fruitful and multiply and prosper you so that He will cause you to pour into many lives. The Lord says you are the head and not the tail and others will serve you. Fear the Lord, and diligently keep his statues, so that you and your sons' sons' days will be prolonged on the earth.

I Love You,

Dad

You may be saying, "well, my dad didn't do that for me", or "my father has passed away and I don't have that opportunity". Nothing could be further from the truth, because you have a heavenly Father who has written an entire book of blessing for you.

Here are some scriptures you can print out and frame and hang in a room somewhere to remind you to receive your father's inheritance.

For I know the plans I have for you, declares the Lord, plans to prosper you and not to harm you, plans to give you hope and a future. Jeremiah 29:11(NIV)

For I command you today to love the Lord your God, to walk in obedience to him, and to keep his commands, decrees and laws; then you will live and increase, and the Lord your God will bless you in the land you are entering to possess. Deuteronomy 30:16 (NIV)

Whoever gives heed to instruction prospers, and blessed is the one who trusts in the Lord. Proverbs 16:20 (NIV)

The blessing of the Lord brings wealth, and he adds no trouble to it. Proverbs 10:22 (NIV)

Do not be wise in your own eyes; fear the Lord and shun evil. This will bring health to your body and nourishment to your bones. Proverbs 3:7-8 (NIV)

The tongue has the power of life and death, and those who love it will eat its fruit. Proverbs 18:21(NIV)

Chapter Eighteen
I have Supernatural Power

"A man's own folly ruins his life, yet his heart rages against the Lord." Proverbs 19:3 (NIV)

People question or blame God for things that have gone wrong in their life, when often they did something that caused a domino effect in their life bringing that specific circumstance or consequence upon them. This isn't the case every time, because yes—bad things do happen to good people. Sometimes we experience severe consequences of sin. We do reap what we sow, so when confronted with a bad outcome, we should examine our lives, including our thought-life, words and actions.

This self-examination has become one of the central themes in my life. The new-ager will call it karma and talk about the universe's influence on us, because their goal is to replace God. If they only would pick up their Bible and read it instead of reading new age philosophy they would see their theory is Biblical and the devil stole it and is trying to take credit for it. Opening a door like this to the dark world can be dangerous. Most people who don't believe the Bible have actually probably never read the Bible. It's amazing how many experts on the Bible there are who have never actually read it. When people read the Bible it becomes alive and changes lives.

Sometimes the adversary attacks because when we turned our

back on him and chose God's way. In this case, we have to fight the good fight of faith as the word tells us. But many times, if we seriously searched our memories and asked God to reveal our shortcomings, we would find that we spoke or acted foolishly as described in the Book of Proverbs, "folly", which means foolishness and lack of good sense.

Many times it's not even an outward act, but an inward act. Men get angry with their wife and hold anger inside that they are not even aware of, which in turn creates animosity and strife in their relationship. Other examples may be spending too much time on the internet or Facebook at work and then wondering why we got fired for lack of performance. Some people will even get bullied due to their own foolishness. They may open their mouth and say something that angers someone and that person then takes it out on them.

Bottom line, friend, is we have supernatural abilities which we have not tapped into yet–all of us! John 14:20 (NIV) says: *"On that day you will realize that I am in my Father, and you are in me, and I am in you."* We were not only created in the image of Almighty God, but He lives inside us. When we walk in love and *"acknowledge that Jesus is the son of God, God lives in him and he in God"* *I John 4:15 (NIV)*. Not only does this scripture say we get eternal life, which makes us immortal in a sense, but He also says that we can receive anything we ask!

Dr. Caroline Leaf [11] talks about how toxic thoughts in our minds are an actual physical thing. Microscopic pictures of thoughts create images that look like trees, demonstrating that proteins and enzymes bloom like a plant. When someone is depressed, sick, angry, or has other toxic thoughts or grudges, these thought trees begin to wilt and look dead, resembling wilted thorn bushes.

---

[11] Dr Caroline. Leaf, 2013, Switch on Your Brain, The Key to Peak Happiness, Thinking and Health, Baker Books

Fortunately we can renew the "spirit" of our minds and reverse this with positive affirmations and prayer. When we say aloud and tell these toxic thoughts of anger, lust, fear, or whatever to leave our mind, they will leave and we can experience freedom. Dr. Leaf believes these toxic thoughts are directly related to physical, emotional, and mental illness and that up to 98% of these infirmities are the direct results of our thinking. I agree with her. The great news is it's not too late to reverse this and experience an abundant life that God has planned for us!

Interesting scriptures support this:

> "If you do not remain in me, you are like a <u>branch</u> that is thrown away and <u>withers</u>; such branches are picked up, thrown into the fire and burned. If you remain in me and my words remain in you, ask whatever you wish, and it will be done for you." John 15; 6-7 (NIV)

> "… but the righteous will thrive like a green leaf." Proverbs 11:28 (NIV)

> "A heart at peace gives life to the body, but envy rots the bones." Proverbs 14:30 (NIV)

> "The tongue that brings healing is <u>a tree of life</u>" Proverbs 15:4 (NIV)

> "I went past the field of a sluggard, past the vineyard of someone who has no sense; <u>thorns had come up everywhere</u>, the ground was covered with <u>weeds,</u> and the stone wall was in ruins. I applied my heart to what I observed and learned a lesson from what I saw: A little sleep, a little slumber, a little folding of the hands

to rest and poverty will come on you like a thief and scarcity like an armed man." Proverbs 24:30-34 (NIV)

*"**The righteous will flourish like a palm tree**, they will grow like a cedar of Lebanon; planted in the house of the Lord, they will flourish in the courts of our God. They will still bear fruit in old age, they will stay fresh and green, proclaiming, "The Lord is upright; he is my Rock, and there is no wickedness in him." Psalms 92:12-15 (NIV)*

*"That person is like a **tree** planted by streams of water, which yields its fruit in season and whose leaf does not wither-- whatever they do prospers." Psalms 1:3(NIV)*

"Thorns and snares are in the way of the perverse; He who guards himself will be far from them." Proverbs 22:5 (NAS)

This particular scripture talks about thorns, which is a similar image of the toxic thoughts in our brain and what they physically look like.

Think of it this way: there are stickers poking into your skull when you think negatively.

This toxic, harmful substance can cause sickness, disease, emotional, and mental damage. You can begin the reversal process right now. Scripture tells us to keep our soul far from them.

Our soul is our mind, will, and emotions. What are you thinking right now? You can overcome toxic thinking. Visualize good things happening to you. Imagine what it will be like when you make that extra money from a bonus or tax refund and the vacation you'll take with your family. Visualize helping others who need financial help or an encouraging word to get them through the tough time they may be facing. Imagine owning your own business or writing that book you've wanted to write. The possibilities of good, healthy thoughts are endless.

Let me propose this to you: those same thorns of toxic thoughts were taken from your mind and place upon Jesus as a crown of thorns when he sacrificed His life for you. *"And the soldiers twisted together a crown of thorns and put it on His head, and put a purple robe on Him" John 19:6(NASB).* Christ already took these toxic thoughts and their consequences for you, so why put it back on to inflict pain and suffering in your life?

Renewal starts with your words, thoughts and what you imagine. One version says, *"He who guards his lips, guards his soul (mind, will, and emotion) Proverbs 13:3 (NIV)."* How do we guard our mind? Fill it up and keep it busy with the things of God. Get involved with something positive. What are your dreams, hobbies, desires? God puts desires in our heart so that we would pursue them to fulfill our divine destiny and calling in life. Don't be one of these people who sit in front of the television every night only to find out your life has just flashed before you with nothing to show for it.

We must make a conscious choice to live right, change habits, trust God, and love others to activate this power within us. We can't just wake up and say life will be different today because King David wrote a psalm that says so or some preacher told me so. Bad habits must be reversed and new ones put in place and practiced daily. This is the daily affirmations I talk about all the time. Joel 3:10 (NIV) says " ... *let the weak say I am strong."* Why would the weak say they are strong? What Joel was saying was that through God you can be strong even when you don't feel like it. When you have Almighty God and His Spirit the Holy Ghost living in you, there is strength inside of you that is not of yourself. It comes from abiding in the vine and being able to ask anything you wish and receive it as John 15 says.

Quit telling yourself "this is the best it's going to get" or "I'm not going anywhere in this job." You must stop the constant wallowing in depression and self-pity and recognize you have God inside you! Think of it this way - When you accept Christ, your DNA is altered and is activated into a powerful force that can defeat the strongholds of the devil and generational curses plaguing your life and your family's life.

"In the paths of the wicked are snares and pitfalls, but those who would preserve their life stay far from them." Proverbs 22:5 (NIV)

Our mind is a power plant of energy that most of us have never even tapped into yet. Our thoughts are actual physical substances that have creative power to transform and change our destiny when utilized properly. The energy from our thoughts can leave our bodies and change the world around us for better or worse. The new-ager and Universalist have figured this out, so why hasn't the body of Christ? We are living underneath our privileges. Which will you choose - life or death, health or sickness, poverty or riches? Create a healthy and prosperous life through your thinking and start right now!

Remember the story about George Bailey the banker in the movie "It's a Wonderful Life" I mentioned in a prior chapter? What if you had never been born? What would life be like for your family and friends who have not had the awesome opportunity to spend time with you and develop relationships with you? Knowing what you now know, that you are a powerful force that has been wonderfully made and possess the DNA of the creator of the universe, how might you change the things that aren't going the greatest in your life ot in the lives of those around you? Could you extend more kindness and love to see the hurting restored? Are there different decisions you can make even today as you read this book? Do you need to release anger toward someone; maybe a friend or spouse or neighbor that upset you?

I invite you right now to activate the supernatural power inside of you by thinking positive and life giving thoughts. Take this truth today and improve your life or the life of someone else and begin to experience inner calm, joy and blessings.

Maybe you already know what change you want to pursue. Perhaps the Lord has been talking to you for a while now, and you simply didn't know where to start. Stop wondering how it's going to happen and take the first step to make it happen. The only person who can truly stop you is you. You are a powerful force full of potential and greatness. Stand up and walk into the new dimension Almighty God has prepared for you!

Chapter Nineteen
The Prayer of Prayers

"Confess your faults one to another, and pray one for another, that ye maybe healed. The effectual fervent prayer of a righteous man availeth much." James 5:16 (KJV)

The effectual fervent prayer of a righteous man has been taught on many times. But what I continue to observe in today's churches with all the seeker sensitive church models is far from effectual or fervent. Effectual has to do with being effective and getting results. Many times we pray and see nothing happen, and we give up. Fervent has to do with being intense and passionate about something. I wish I would hear more Christians pray like they cheer for their home team at a football or baseball game. Effective and fervent prayer should at least come close or equal the energy and passion of our support for an athletic event.

I'm not saying we shouldn't also pray quietly. There is a time and a place for that. In fact, Scripture tells us to go into our prayer closet, and the Bible cautions us against praying so that others can see and hear us and thus consider us more righteous. When we are thanking God or just having a conversation with Him it might be an appropriate time for that style of prayer.

However, when we are in an all-out battle with the devil and we want to see results, we must be passionate and pray with the goal of achieving certain results in our minds. It reminds me of parents with unruly and dysfunctional children. They try to reason with the child, saying things like "now Johnny, that's not very nice to hit mommy like that." And then they wonder why their kids get into so much trouble in school and have no discipline in their life. Friend, if you want results, you have got to become more passionate and fervent! You're fighting the devil and he is out to kill, steal, and destroy you.

The devil is the biggest bully of all, and we must learn to stand up to him and defeat him with the power we have been given. Matthew 16:19 (NIV) says *"I will give you the keys of the kingdom of heaven; whatever you bind on earth will be bound in heaven, and whatever you loose on earth will be loosed in heaven."* We underestimate the power we have. God Almighty is living in us. We can speak to the mountains and the bullies of life and see them move. Loose that sickness and poverty mentality and bind health and prosperity to your life.

I remember a time when I was just out of college and couldn't find a job in the specific area of my degree. I looked all over, constantly sending out my resume and diligently applying for various positions to support my wife and young son. I was working two and three jobs to make ends meet. I wasn't getting enough sleep during this time and experienced sleep deprivation, which led to stress and anxiety and having panic attacks.

I'll never forget an instance where I woke up in the middle of the night in a panic attack and felt like I was losing my mind. It's hard to explain what it's like without actually experiencing it. I felt overwhelming guilt, confusion, and fear. I trembled with fear and absolute terror. It was about 3:00 in the morning, and the only thing I could think of to do was call my dad, because he understood how to pray fervently. Some may make fun of the old time Pentecostal saints, but you can't take away the fact that they know how to touch the throne of God and see results.

When I called and explained what I was dealing with, my voice trembling, he immediately went into aggressive intersession. He spoke with great authority and demanded the evil spirit of fear and anxiety to leave. He bound the attack against me and prayed in the spirit. In less than five minutes, I relaxed and felt complete freedom and peace come over me. I believe if he had spoken in a very passive tone, saying something like "Lord, just help David relax and not think about all the stressful things he is facing." I would not have experienced the same supernatural release. His effectual fervent prayer was heard and answered! When we are in a fight with the adversary of our soul we have got to speak up and demand him to stop his attack!

When we appropriate the power God has given us in the name of His Son Jesus, we can do supernatural acts. Jesus told us that we would do greater things than He did because He was going to the Father. He gave us the Holy Ghost to give us understanding to deal with the cares of life and the attacks of the enemy. The scripture states that we will be given power after the Holy Ghost comes upon us. That power allows us to defeat the evil one and have complete freedom from terror.

Too often we take a backseat to the evil forces of darkness and cave in. Then we wonder why we lose so many battles. The devil bullies us first in our mind. We let our mind wander and it gets us into trouble with doubt and unbelief. Be disciplined in your thought life. Think about what you're thinking about all the time. Because of being bullied as a young boy, later in life I was always defensive, thinking everyone was out to take advantage of me or were always critical. Your self-worth and self-esteem are tainted when you allow yourself to think like this. Remember your identity is not who you are, but who you are related to. Who is your father? You are made in the very image of your father the Almighty Creator, Jehovah Elohim

Adonai, and Yahweh – the majestic all-knowing God. You are not just a banker, doctor, teacher, grocery store clerk or policeman. You are more than a mere human, but have the glory of God inside of you!

There are times we have to summon the angels of the Lord to go out and fight on our behalf. When we pray, God disperses them on our behalf, but I have seen even more effective prayers when we specifically ask for help from the heavenly host. Not that we should pray to angels, but they do serve us. We must always ask the Father in Jesus' name, because that is the key to effective prayers and seeing results. If we expect to dismiss the bullies from our life, we must begin seeing ourselves as Super Heroes. We have been given the keys to live in the supernatural realm and to walk in greatness.

The scripture in Romans 10:9 (NIV) says: "If you declare with your mouth, 'Jesus is Lord' and believe in your heart that God raised him from the dead, you will be saved." Usually this scripture is used to teach unbelievers how to receive "eternal" salvation from hell. This scripture, along with John 3:16, tells us how to be saved, but it goes further than that.

If you find yourself in a situation with a bully of life terrorizing and threatening you, state out loud, "Jesus is Lord and God has raised Him from the dead" and watch what happens. Your Heavenly Father will step in and *save* you from that bad situation when you declare Christ is Lord. We can use this in crises to call upon our Creator and ask Him to send forth his angelic army to come and reverse the situation. He will save you when you call upon His Name and declare to the adversary that He is Lord and was raised from the dead.

Many people worry about what others will think of them if they raise their voice a little to the devil, but when someone runs them off the road or their team scores points, they sure are not quiet. Quit worrying about what others may think and start telling the devil he has no right to your children, your marriage, or your money.

God can grant you an inner peace knowing that all will be okay because you are transformed by the renewing of your mind. Start commanding the blessings of God to overtake your finances and for supernatural favor to be given to you with everyone you meet. Put a shield of protection around your family and your marriage so that attacks which come your way will not even be noticeable. We can bind the forces of hell in our prayers and loose the abundant life Jesus promised to us. Let's start doing that now!

It will take time for change, so we must be consistent in our behavior. The word says in "due season" or at the "right time" we will reap if we don't faint or lose hope. That means it may take some time, but don't give up. We must make a conscious effort to examine our thought life every day. The choice is ours to make. Start now and get out of that bad cycle and addictive habits that control your life. Check your thoughts right now. Check them when you wake in the morning and when you go to sleep at night. Life is about choices. How we make those choices will determine the outcome of our final destiny.

When we exhibit godly character, He releases His power and provision in our life. We must check our moral compass and ask God to show us how to break the barriers and strongholds in our life that hold us back. When we search the word of God, He will speak through His word into our situation and circumstance. Dealing with our heart issues allows God to mold us the way He wants.

Many diseases and sicknesses are the direct results of our heart. Do you have bitterness, anger, jealousy, or fear? Ask the Holy Spirit to reveal to you hidden shame, hurts, or pains of the past so that you can loose them. God longs to set you free, but you also have a part in this. Many people like to take the passive path and say that God will work it out. Yes, of course He does in His own time. But we have been injected with power from on high.

In the movie about Captain America, he was injected with a substance that made him powerful. Think of yourself as injected with supernatural healing and miraculous power that enable you to take on anything that comes your way. Captain America could jump over high fences and shield off the bullets of the enemy. He was stronger than any of the soldiers he fought. Begin to see yourself like this. Visualize the devil and his demonic forces running in terror when you walk in a room or begin to pray for someone. I used to have terror, anxiety and stress, now I cause the devil to have terror, anxiety and stress. He doesn't keep me up at night – I keep him up!

I love the stories of super heroes, especially Superman and Captain America. They were men of high moral character and integrity that was woven into their innermost fiber. They protected others and fought off the enemy. They weren't passive and timid, but they exhibited strength and power. Though they may have gotten knocked down, they always got up stronger and braver with an extra dose of energy. That's how we need to be. Even when we feel knocked down, we must learn to get up on the inside and fight the devil with the word of God built into our prayers.

> *"For though a righteous man falls seven times, and rises again, but the wicked are brought down by their calamity." Proverbs 24:16 (NIV)*

People say, "I'm sick and tired" of something or another. Is that really what you want? Why are you speaking that over yourself? Why not get sick and tired of being "sick and tired" and quit saying that? Words are powerful, and so much of what we say we don't even think about. Words create things in our life, as do our thoughts. I have caught myself saying this and immediately think, "NO". I renounce that phrase and reject that curse over my life. Be self-aware of your thoughts and words.

There was a time I was being bullied very badly and thoughts of suicide came into my mind. I felt that was the only way out. There was such a feeling of hopelessness because I felt I would never be accepted. I was fat, unattractive, and insecure. I was going nowhere in life. At least that's what I thought.

Being rejected hurts and wounds you in your deepest parts and make you feel unwanted and lost. Suicide is selfish and devastates others left behind. It's not the solution and should never be an option.

Emotional freedom can come only through Christ and prayer. You can mask stress, depression, and hurt with medication, but only the power of God Almighty can bring you complete freedom and restoration. Visualize that you are a super hero inside and nothing can overcome you. You have been given a great gift from God in the Holy Spirit which grants you supernatural power. It pumps you up like Superman is living inside you, and nothing will defeat you!

Pray every day. Use the Lord's Prayer as the basis of how you pray. Calling forth Heaven to come down to earth will change your situation. Use the blood of Jesus and speak with authority at your adversity. You have the keys to the Kingdom to create a new environment in your life. Don't let the devil discourage you and do not dwell on the thoughts he tries to put in your mind. Focus on positive thoughts and meditate daily on scripture. Then implement scripture in your prayer life and watch the circumstances change in your favor!

At the end of the day, you cannot always expect others to provide protection against bullies in life for you, whether they are school teachers, counselors, pastors, the school principle, attorneys, human resources, or even law enforcement. They cannot be there for you all the time. One young man I mentored who was being bullied was caught walking alone on the street. There was nobody there to protect him. Bullies beat him up and he had to spend time at the hospital. I encouraged him to pray in those times, which he was not doing. I told him of the powerful force of prayer and how God could send angels to protect him. So many times however we just don't remember and forget who is on our side.

Our only source of absolute protection is our Heavenly Father. When we ask Him for protection, He will grant it. That doesn't include covering your hot temper or smart mouth. This doesn't mean you can't stand up for yourself, just don't be the instigator. The power of prayer in situations with bullies can bring protection. Declare that, "Jesus is Lord and God raised Him from the dead" and watch Him step in and work and fight on your behalf.

As an adult, I had a boss who was a bully. When we went to loan committee, he always enjoyed belittling and humiliating people, probably in an attempt to prove he was smarter than everyone else. At least that's what he thought.

A lot of times, bullies have self-esteem issues themselves. Sometimes, they have a sense of entitlement and truly feel they have a right to act that way. One time in loan committee, I arrived early and circled the conference room praying in the Spirit. I commanded the mouth of the bully I knew would be there to be shut. I continued praying and circling the room. I prayed over his chair and spoke silence to his voice. He was a member of loan committee who loved to humiliate others to make himself look better. In the past, he had made female lenders in our bank cry as he abused them verbally. A few minutes into my presentation, someone interrupted and said, "I move for approval" and another immediately spoke up and said, "I second." I looked across the table at the bully and he opened his mouth but nothing came out! Friend, if you don't believe that praying in the Spirit is for today, you are missing out on a powerful tool God has given his children to overcome the world of bullies and evil! Read the books of Acts, Ephesians, and I Corinthians. There are sometimes we do not know how to pray, so we must rely on the Holy Ghost to help us.

"In the same way, the Spirit helps us in our weakness.
We do not know what we ought to pray for, but the

Spirit himself intercedes for us through wordless groans." Romans 8:26 (NIV)

Best kept secret

The devil cannot intercept prayers that we pray in the Spirit or what some refer to as praying in an unknown tongue. As mentioned in a previous chapter, that gift was given to us freely, but many don't want to accept that powerful and wonderful gift Jesus gave because of fear and incorrect Biblical interpretation. Don't allow your blessing of a gift from God to be restricted to status quo. Often the only way to get your answers and the freedom you are looking for is through praying in the Spirit. No one understands it completely, and I am not even going to try to explain it theologically except to say that it works!

> *"But the natural man receiveth not the things of the Spirit of God: for they are foolishness unto him: neither can he know them, because they are spiritually discerned." I Corinthians 2:14 (KJV)*

The power of praying in the Spirit is one of the best kept secrets in Christianity. I say secrets because most churches are not teaching this any more as a form of spiritual warfare. The sad part of it is, many Christians have not even read their Bible and studied this section Paul where talks about it. Many don't believe it is for today, but they also don't know how to walk in complete power. Miracles, signs, and wonders are there for the taking, but to summon them up you must be walking in the spirit.

> *"For anyone who speaks in a tongue does not speak to men but to God. Indeed no one understands him;*

he utters mysteries with his spirit." I Corinthians 14:2 (NIV)

The Apostle Paul says he wishes everyone would speak in tongues, but the reality is that many deny this gift because of fear or unbelief. Praying in your God-given Heavenly language is another weapon in our arsenal against the devil, so don't leave the gift on the table and walk out. Do you want to move up to a higher dimension with Almighty God? Ask Him to fill you with His Holy Spirit, and He will give it to you, and it will include the gift of praying in the Spirit and the gift of speaking in tongues that can change the course of your life!

I have seen multiple times how this weapon of praying in the Spirit changes circumstance. You can expect favor, health, prosperity, restoration in your marriage, salvation to your children. Begin to experience the very best God has for your life. He calls this a gift, so why wouldn't you accept a gift, especially if it is something you can use to live a supernatural blessed life?

Chapter Twenty
Destiny Fulfilled

"The Lord will fulfill his purpose for me; your steadfast love, O Lord, endures forever" Psalms 138:8 (ESV)

We're all farmers.

Sowing seed was something I learned growing up in the farmlands of Wisconsin. We didn't live on a farm, but farmers attended my dad's church, and we had a garden on our three acres that seemed like a farm, especially when us four kids had to pull weeds in the hot Wisconsin humidity with swarms of mosquitos flying around. Add to that the hay fever allergies I suffered with as a young man. There's no wonder I don't want to have a garden today! I actually enjoy fresh vegetables from the garden; I just don't like the upkeep!

We planted corn, green beans, tomatoes, carrots, watermelons, radishes, and probably several other vegetables that I didn't get too excited about as a kid. Today I appreciate them more than I did back then. One of my fondest memories is coming in from playing or doing chores and smelling fresh green beans or corn on the cob cooking in Mom's kitchen. We also had fruit trees –apple and plum, and Mom made jelly and canned it. We kept canned goods in the basement, or what many referred to in that day as the "cellar."

The first year we planted that huge 40-acre garden (well, maybe not 40 acres—it just felt like it) and watching the plants sprout. Where we planted corn seed, corn stalks grew. Where we planted potatoes, potato plants grew. What you planted is what you reaped.

This holds true for the rest of our life. In the vast garden of life in this world, if you harbor bitterness and anger, that's exactly what your life will be like and no one will want to be around you. You'll grow old and wonder why your kids, family, and friends won't come to visit.

My dad was always joyful and had a smile on his face. He radiated with the joy of the Lord and loved to joke around, often telling the same joke 50 times or more. But folks didn't seem to mind. They wanted to be around my dad. He brought joy into their lives. He was positive and thought the best of people. If you plant joy into the lives of others, you'll reap a harvest of joy, happiness and fulfillment in your life in return.

You can pray until you are blue in the face, quotes scriptures in your prayers, and cast the devil out of every door handle you bump into, but unless you are planting good seeds of kindness, meekness, humility, selflessness, and a giving heart, you will struggle feeling fulfilled. If you're a bully to people, trust me—your day is coming. There will be a reckoning! There is a harvest time where things come back to you. What you have done to others will be done to you. You reap what you sow and if you sow nothing, that's exactly what you'll receive.

> *"Do not be deceived: God cannot be mocked. A man reaps what he sows. Whoever sows to please their flesh, from the flesh will reap destruction; whoever sows to please the Spirit, from the Spirit will reap eternal life." Galatians 6:7-8 (NIV)*

This principle works in our finances as well. Some say that tithing is an Old Testament law and tradition which is not mentioned much in the New Testament, but the principle holds true. It is a law of nature and of God that when you put a seed in the ground, something comes up. If you give to your church, non-profits, widows, the homeless, and the fatherless, the Bible says you will lack nothing.

It's a heart issue. I know folks who give tithes and still struggle. Most of the time, it's because of their attitude and frivolous spending habits. You must use wisdom in the area of giving and do what the Lord tells you to do. Please don't let yourself be manipulated in your giving, but allow to the Holy Spirit to instruct you in this matter.

God's plan for your life is to live abundantly and in health, but we do have a choice in this matter. You can't ask God to give health and healing but then choose to abuse your body by smoking, overeating, drinking to excess, and never exercising. God's plan is for us to use wisdom in every area of our life and enjoy it to the fullest.

"There is surely a future hope for you, and your hope will not be cut off. "Proverbs 23:18(NIV)

I know what it's like to struggle in the area of finances and health. Living from paycheck to paycheck is not fun, and dealing with constant illness can steal your joy and zap your strength. When you learn to give to others, take care of yourself, and honor everyone, you will see circumstances change for the better.

"For the flesh desires what is contrary to the Spirit, and the Spirit what is contrary to the flesh. They are in conflict with each other, so that you are not to do whatever you want." Galatians 5:17 (NIV)

If we want to experience kingdom living here on earth, we must say no to the flesh. That may mean not eating that second piece of cake or maybe not eating the first piece if your sugar level is too high. If you get nervous all the time and have anxiety, limit yourself to one cup of coffee instead of the whole pot. Or try caffeine-free teas or another type of beverage you enjoy. Saying no may mean less time on Facebook, or perhaps fewer online or computer games. Integrity is doing the right thing when no one is looking. That's where the blessing lies. You're the stronger person when you say no and avoid evil, instead choosing to invest back into the kingdom.

You may say "what does this have to do with bullies?" It has everything to do with them. Don't bully anyone and you have a better chance of not being bullied yourself. When you honor God and treat people with love, kindness, and respect, you'll reap a better harvest in return. Our flesh wants to retaliate when we are confronted, and I'm not saying don't defend yourself. The Bible tells us that a soft answer turns away wrath. There is such peace and tranquility in knowing that no matter what comes your way, you can be safe and content in Christ.

Many diseases stem from environmental issues or poor food choices, but that's not the only causes. Much of our suffering is rooted in spiritual and emotional issues. Learning to break generational curses including being bullied, divorce, cancer, heart disease, anger, jealousy, and financial lack can be appropriated when we pray and use the Name and blood of Jesus. Sometime we open doors to darkness that puts evil upon us through what we watch on TV, what books we read, what music we listen to, and what sites we visit on the Internet.

And the Internet is a particularly insidious trap our adversary the devil tries to snare us in. When we look at something inappropriate on the Internet, we extend an open invitation for evil to come into our home and our life. This harm could affect even our spouse and children.

If the devil himself was standing at your door with a plate of chocolate cookies, and they looked like the best cookies you had ever seen, would you let him in? Of course not because you and I both know he has a motive to bring destruction. Yet we don't make that same connection when it comes to what our eyes take in. Our eyes are the windows of our soul and what we see with them can bring blessings or curses.

When you sit up late watching horrors movies, you give the powers of evil the right to come in and bring fear and worry into your home. We must be conscious of everything to which we expose ourselves. Music and books are another way to expose yourself to evil. Anything we listen to often enough becomes our truth.

I know you might be thinking I'm crazy stating this. Well, let me tell you, my family and I live in almost perfect health and financial prosperity. Does the enemy attack? Sure, he does. That's his job, to kill, steal, and destroy, but we are supernaturally blessed. Recognizing the traps the enemy of our soul lays before us is critical to achieving kingdom living here on earth. After we realize what he is up to, we must make a decision to submit to God and the Word says he (the devil) will flee from you.

Lay a good foundation in your home with prayer every morning. Offer thanks for all that you have been given and cover your family with the blood of Jesus just like the children of Israel did in Egypt as the death angel came through the camp to destroy the firstborn. When the devil sees the blood, he will pass over you because he knows you are a child of the most high God and have been redeemed by the blood of the lamb. We do this by speaking the blood of Jesus over ourselves.

In order to take advantage of this kingdom life, you must first recognize the way to God. That is only through his Son Jesus Christ who paid the penalty for your sin. The Bible says: *"If you declare with your mouth, 'Jesus is Lord,' and believe in your heart that God raised him from the dead, you will be saved." Romans 10:9 (NIV)*

Oh you can have riches and health without God and His Son Jesus, but your wealth and health will never fill the void in your life. Fulfillment only comes with an intimate relationship with God. It's all a heart issue. It's about your motives. You can have a successful business, be a rich entertainer, a great sports hero, or pastor a megachurch, but if your heart isn't right and pure before God, you will not experience the true peace and everlasting joy that only comes from knowing the Lord.

> *"Surely the arm of the LORD is not too short to save, nor his ear too dull to hear. But your iniquities have separated you from your God; your sins have hidden his face from you, so that he will not hear." Isaiah 59:1-2 (NIV)*

You cannot expect blessing and joy to fall into your lap. There will be fights with the evil one, I guarantee it. But you are an overcomer by the blood of the Lamb and the word of your testimony. All things are possible with God and you have His Spirit living in you, which makes you His child with a great inheritance. You usually have to wait until someone dies before you can get your inheritance, but Jesus Christ, the only living Son of God, already died for you and you can walk in favor, financial prosperity, divine health, joy, peace, and blessing everywhere we go.

Have you made a covenant with the devil?

I've asked this before, and I'll ask it again: how are you thinking? What are you saying in your mind? Fear starts in the mind and is the root of so many of our problems. The devil tells us lies and then we believe it and COME INTO COVENANT with him! We make ourselves vulnerable to the bullies of life because of fear. Choose right now to come into covenant with God's word. *"Perfect love casteth out fear"* the word of God says. *I John 4:18 (KJV)*

We walk in love when we abide in God, because He is the very essence of love. When we love and honor others, we can walk in true victory. Begin to see things the way they are in the spirit realm. The devil brings fear due to the lies he tells us. When we allow that fear to grip our hearts, the evil one has already won half the battle. Once we re-program our minds and begin to speak his word and declare positive affirmation and believe it in our hearts so much that we can smell our new home or the new car we need, Gods act on our behalf.

Don't listen to the lies the devil tells you. You are the redeemed, which means it's like you never sinned in the first place. It's like you are put in the position of a newborn baby that has never sinned. That's how God sees you through the blood of Jesus His Son. Start seeing yourself the same way. Don't allow the devil to control your life any further. Take charge and stand up to him because he is the worst bully around.

When we dwell on the negative circumstances, they begin to manifest in many ways that can result in shame and guilt as well as vain imaginations. The Bible tells us to take wrong thoughts captive. Whatever we bind on earth will be bound in Heaven. There is no fear, sickness, shame, poverty, or bitterness in Heaven. That's what we can experience here on earth. Draw close to God and don't wait till devastation, sickness, accident, or job loss comes before deciding to make some changes–do it now! Fear will manifest in disease, sickness, worry, anxiety, anger, and lack in many areas of our life including finances.

God is ready to restore today if you are ready to receive it. Put your hands out right now and say "God, I receive restoration in my life, in my marriage, in my finances, in my children, and in every area of my life." Say, "I close the doors that I have opened through which I brought forth evil into my life. I close the doors I've opened unaware. I seal them forever in the blood of Jesus. I repent and renounce all sin in my life and reverse the curse and break every generation curse from my father, forefathers, and people who have influence over me. I remove all toxic thoughts and desires from my thinking and lay them at the cross of Jesus. I declare I am free, favored, healthy, and wealthy so I can help to advance the Kingdom of God. Amen"

You do have a part in this. You can't just sit back and expect Santa Claus Jesus to give you everything you ask. You must step out in faith and believe what the word of God says, plant positive seeds around you, expect the best and not the worst. Examine what you are exposing yourself to and immediately stop all negativity.

The book of Hosea says in chapter 4 verse 6 that God's people perish for lack of knowledge. I pray this book will impart some wisdom so that you have additional physical and spiritual knowledge for dealing with bullies you may be facing. God can intercept the bullies in every area of your life. We can call on Him and he will answer when we are living right, honoring and loving Him. We have a part, my friend, and sometimes it doesn't come without paying a price, but that's the easy part because Jesus already paid the price in full and bought us with the greatest price ever paid.

Everyone has a story. You may be facing a bully in your life right now that seems too big to fight. It may be a sickness, or a disease, or financial difficulty. Your marriage may be on the verge of divorce or you may have a spouse who has been unfaithful. God can restore, but we all have choices to make. We can believe and move forward with our lives or allow ourselves to be depressed and bitter.

Everyone has a story.

The great news is you hold the pen in your hand to finish the book of the story of your life. How will it end? Step out in faith and pursue the goals, dreams, and desires God has put in your heart. They are not in your heart by accident. He wants to advance His kingdom and use you for his glory and divine purpose.

The scripture says in Matthew 18:18 (NIV) *"Truly I tell you, whatever you bind on earth will be bound in heaven, and whatever you loose on earth will be loosed in heaven."* The ultimate key of authority to achieve what we want in life lines up with God's plan and purpose. It's time to loose off the bully who has been terrorizing and mistreating you, whether that's a classmate, former friend, boss, or relative. It may even be a sickness; a generational curse of poverty; bitterness; or anger in your life. Start binding healthy relationships, protection, and favor to yourself.

When you begin to think this way and talk this way to yourself, you will begin to see blessings overtake your life. Start seeing yourself as the champion God created you to be. You are not defeated, but are an overcomer. You can do all things through Christ who strengthens you. If the same spirit that raised Christ from the dead is in you, as the word of God declares, nothing can defeat you unless you allow it. Even in difficult times, put a smile on your face, remember all that you have, and be grateful. With a thankful heart and through praise and worshipping the true God Yahweh, heaven will come to earth and the bullies of life will be defeated before you.

Steps to Success

- Pray daily and use the Lord's Prayer
- Daily positive affirmations over your life and family
- Pray with your spouse every day (if you're married)
- Read your Bible daily – don't compromise this – make it habit as this is how we hear God's voice many times speaking to us
- Avoid confrontations with bullies. Remember: a soft answer turns away wrath
- Renew the spirit of your mind daily. Literally say "I remove the thoughts of suicide from my mind" or "I remove the thoughts of fear of being bullied"
- Use scripture in your prayer life and when talking to yourself
  - *Greater is He that is in me than he that is in the world*
  - *I can do all things through Christ who strengthens me*
  - *The same spirit that raised Christ from the dead is in me*
  - *I am more than a conqueror*

- o *Jesus is Lord and God raised Him from the dead* (you will be saved)
- Break off past generational curses
- Learn to pray in the spirit – read the Book of Acts (this is powerful!)
- Use the blood of Jesus when praying to cover yourself with protection
- Stop sinning – you reap what you sow
- Remove low self-esteem – see yourself as a champion, hold your head up high
- Eat right and exercise, try a salad instead of a burger once in a while, and get out and walk. Set the IPhone down, turn off the TV, and quit wasting your life away. Go for a walk, jog, or hike, and lighten up
- Take deep breaths and trust God will work it out when you are doing your best

Take the ideas and examples I have mentioned in this book and begin to apply them to your life. There is no secret recipe for everything to always go perfect, but there are some actions we can take to get a reaction and to live a more fulfilled life of abundant joy and inner peace. Start now and enjoy the journey of life God has promised you. Make the decision in your heart to accept what a great price God paid for you by giving His Son Jesus to secure your eternal life. Trust in the Lord with all your heart and in a short time you will see His mighty hand at work in your life.

Sources

1. Dr. Caroline Leaf, Switch On Your Brain, Baker Books, 2013
2. Henry Wright, *A More Excellent Way*, Whitacker House March, 10, 2009

3. Janet Maccaro, PhD, *Breaking the Grip of Dangerous Emotions,* Siloam A Strang Company 2001, 2005

4. Most scripture was sourced from The Holy Bible, New International Version 1978 by New York International Bible Society AKA New York Bible Society. Other scriptures and their versions were used from http://biblehub.com/